MW00569623

Washington Villa
A South Boston
Neighborhood Rediscovered

By Richard Kennedy and Bennie DiNardo

CORE
INVESTMENTS, INC.

Core Investments, Inc.
David Pogorelc, Founder
May 2020

WASHINGTON VILLAGE: A SOUTH BOSTON NEIGHBORHOOD REDISCOVERED

Contents

Color maps of Washington Village after Page 60.

Foreword

Thank you for selecting this book on Washington Village!

Washington Village was a historic neighborhood of Boston that few residents are aware of today—and we are bringing it back. Our company recognized the attractiveness and potential of this part of South Boston a decade ago, as the robust era of industrial use—including familiar names like Crown Uniform and Linen, with its landmark chimney—began to fade or leave the neighborhood.

Long ago, industrial uses shared the blocks with a residential community, and we began conversations right away with families and individuals who called the area home. Together, we recognized that the area once referred to as Washington Village, but more recently considered part of the Andrew Square neighborhood, would undergo change, as neighborhoods unalterably do. But what could it be? What should it be?

As you will read, the triangle of land around today's Dorchester Avenue, Old Colony Avenue, and Dorchester Street in South Boston was largely forgotten for a period after Europeans came to the area in the early 1600s. After cows grazed, it was a transportation corridor—for a brief time for George Washington's army, then for all modes of transportation from horses to, eventually, highways.

Those who inhabited the area early on viewed it as Boston's—and, as it became, the nation's—workshop. It was a major center of the new republic's iron and manufacturing business. It turned out military hardware that protected our freedoms. The factories of the neighborhood created the finest modern excavators and dredges in the world.

WASHINGTON VILLAGE: A SOUTH BOSTON NEIGHBORHOOD REDISCOVERED

What had been a small residential neighborhood expanded to host immigrants and laborers. In the mid-1800s, residents named their area Washington Village, in honor of George Washington's seminal occupation of Dorchester Heights against the British army.

The name "Washington Village" was short-lived. After only a few decades, in 1891, the area was renamed Andrew Square, after the late abolitionist and Civil War governor of Massachusetts, John A. Andrew. Though references to "Washington Village" were found in newspapers into the 1920s, the area gradually became less residential.

But in the twenty-first century, the neighborhood's proximity to the city and easy access to existing transportation options again attracted residential interest.

Today's powerful trend is toward a convenient mix of uses. Residents are attracted to neighborhoods where work may be nearby and where there are restaurants and shops.

Current Washington Village residents and new ones will live, work, and enjoy life here, the legacy of a rich history and the result of thoughtful planning. All will benefit from its location and the extraordinary transportation access that has historically characterized the area.

Welcome to Washington Village. Welcome back, Washington Village.

David Pogorelc, Founder
Core Investments, Inc.

Introduction

The triangle of land in South Boston's southwestern corner—about seventy largely forgotten acres along and around today's Dorchester Avenue, Old Colony Avenue, and Dorchester Street in South Boston—has a rich and varied history.

The low-lying, often flooded neck that connected the South Boston peninsula to the mainland to the south was overlooked for much of the time after Europeans began to colonize the area in the early 1600s. It was a place to pass through, when conditions permitted, from one destination to another—first for pasturing cows, then for a brief time for George Washington's army, then for all modes of transportation from horses to streetcars to railroads to subways to highways. Even before European settlement, Native Americans used the land only occasionally, visiting during the warmer months to fish its waters and dig along its shoreline and mudflats for shellfish.

Those who put down roots in the area viewed it as Boston's—and eventually, America's—workshop. Flat, empty, close to the population and commercial activity of Boston and its harbor, reachable by land and water from Boston to the north and the growing communities of Dorchester and its southern neighbors, the area sprouted factories, furnaces, and foundries, and became a major center of the new republic's iron and manufacturing business. Cyrus Alger and his foundries produced the ammunition and weapons the federal government relied upon for much of the nineteenth century, from the War of 1812 through the Civil War. The railroad yards that sprang up around South Bay fueled a booming business in locomotive production, and the area's factories responded with the engines that pulled the first train cars across the continent. To help carve out and build the railroads, harbor facilities, canals, and whole

INTRODUCTION

neighborhoods the city and the country were constructing to conquer and connect the continent, these factories of the neighborhood turned out innovation after innovation that made the work possible, including the finest modern excavators and dredges the world had ever seen.

Slowly, a residential neighborhood also developed to house the immigrants and laborers the factories required. First, a small group of no more than a dozen households from Dorchester settled the pastures, orchards, and fields of South Boston, but many were driven out in the preliminary fighting that led up to Washington's surprise occupation of Dorchester Heights at the start of the American Revolution. Near today's Andrew Square, a small cluster of households grew in an area called Little Neck, reaching a population of 1,300 by the middle of the nineteenth century. Far from the meeting house and places of worship in Dorchester and closer to the urban, industrial corridor of South Boston, the residents voted to rename this area Washington Village in 1850, in honor of George Washington's surprise occupation of Dorchester Heights, which forced the British army to evacuate Boston in the first great victory of the American Revolution almost eighty years earlier. In 1855, after several unsuccessful attempts, Washington Village broke away from Dorchester and became part of the city of Boston.

Washington Village existed as an official city neighborhood for just four decades; by 1891, the area was renamed Andrew Square, after the late Civil War governor of Massachusetts, John A. Andrew. Though references to Washington Village can be found in newspapers such as the *Boston Globe* into the 1920s, the area became less residential as transportation projects, including the expansion of subway service to South Boston and Dorchester and the construction of the Southeast Expressway, claimed many homes.

7

The large foundries and factories of the nineteenth century gave way to smaller enterprises in the twentieth—glass shops, auto body shops, construction services, printers, and other industries that provided the skills, tools, and equipment to keep the Boston economy working. Some of those smaller enterprises, such as Crown Uniform and Linen Service, Karas & Karas Glass, and the Marr Companies, became major businesses themselves, employing hundreds and fueling the boom Boston experienced starting at the end of the twentieth century.

In the current century, Boston's population surged as its newer industries—in fields such as high technology, biotechnology, and medical research—brought jobs and residents back to the city. Once again, as happened when the country was young and Boston was looking for ways to expand beyond the small peninsula where it was first settled, the area's proximity to the city and easy access to existing transportation options attracted interest. In 2015, developer Dave Pogorelc proposed resurrecting the area's historic name, Washington Village, and building a residential neighborhood to replace the warehouse, commercial, and industrial buildings in the area with housing and retail, surrounding a village green. As the Mount Vernon Proprietors wrote in their proposal to annex South Boston from Dorchester in 1804:

While the present town [Boston] would always continue the great focus of business, this quarter of it could provide for the surplus of population, and furnish the inhabitants with suitable sites for houses and other buildings, at prices greatly beneath those in the town, which have at length become exorbitant, and consequently detrimental to an increase of new citizens, and discouraging to those arts upon which an infinite variety of trades are dependent.

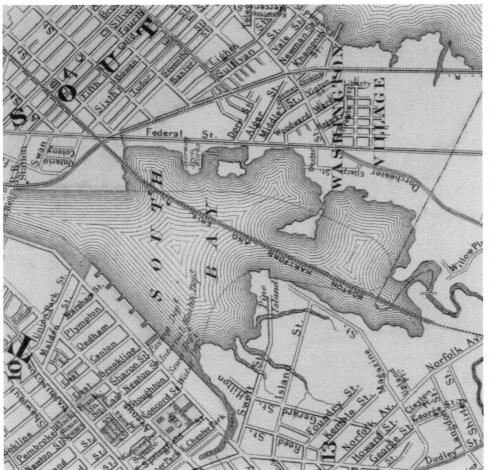

1870. Johnson, A.J. "Boston and vicinity." Map. Detail. *Norman B. Leventhal Map & Education Center.*

Image next page and at following chapters: 1855. Colton, J.H., and J.H. Colton & Co. "Map of Boston and adjacent cities." Map. Detail. *Norman B. Leventhal Map & Education Center.*

Chapter 1. First Contact

As the sixteenth century dawned, the land and waters of present-day New England were teeming with people. On shore, about twenty-five thousand natives organized into multiple tribes—the Wampanoag, the Nauset, and the Massachusett—lived along the coast of Massachusetts and Rhode Island, all speaking variations of the Massachusett language, itself a dialect of Algonquian, which was the dominant language of eastern North America, home to one hundred thousand people or more.

Offshore, waves of Europeans—British, French, Portuguese, and Italians— were fishing the fertile waters and sometimes trading with the natives. By 1610, the British alone had an estimated two hundred ships sailing off the coast of present-day New England and Newfoundland. But most of those sailors and explorers had little interest in inhabiting the new lands they were visiting. The French explorer Samuel de Champlain visited Cape Cod in 1605 and 1606, seeking to establish a base for further French activity in the area; he changed his mind when he saw that too many people lived there already. In 1607, the British explorer Sir Ferdinando Gorges attempted to establish a community in Maine; his party was larger than the one the Pilgrims sent to Plymouth a decade later and was better organized and equipped. But he was driven back by natives who, large in number and well-armed, killed eleven of the would-be colonists before the rest returned to their ships.

But in just ten years, conditions in New England changed drastically. Beginning in 1616, according to Charles C. Mann's *1491: New Revelations of the Americas Before Columbus*, an epidemic that was most likely viral hepatitis, spread by contaminated food, wiped out as much as 90 percent of the native population along the New England coast. Natives "died in heapes as they lay in their houses," the merchant Thomas Morton later observed, describing the forests of Massachusetts as a "new-found Golgotha," a Biblical reference to the Place of the Skull where Jesus and others were crucified.

Across North and South America, the aftermath of the first contact between the peoples of Europe and the Americas was just as deadly. Exposure to diseases previously unknown in the Americas—diseases such as smallpox, typhus, influenza, diphtheria, and measles—wiped out as much as 90 percent of the more than one hundred million inhabitants of the Americas. The estimated death toll of 90 to 112 million people was, according to Mann, more than the population of Europe at the time. Disease claimed a staggering one out of every five people on Earth, he said, "the greatest destruction of lives in human history." "The Black Death that hit Europe during the Middle Ages claimed seventy-five to two hundred million victims, and the worldwide influenza epidemic following World War I also claimed fifty million to one hundred million lives, but neither came close to the estimated death rate of 90 percent that native American populations experienced.

This was the world the Pilgrims encountered when the Mayflower anchored off the coast of Massachusetts in 1620. Tisquantum, the Indian known popularly as Squanto, made his home in Patuxet, the Wampanoag village on the site of present-day Plymouth. He had been captured in 1614 during a visit to the area by Captain John Smith of Jamestown fame. Tisquantum was taken first to Europe, then released to a British fishing camp in Newfoundland, then sailed to Maine. From there, he ultimately decided to walk the rest of the way to Patuxet. What he saw on that journey home was, Mann wrote, "unimaginable." Every settlement along the coast was abandoned, the inhabitants gone. "What had once been a line of busy communities was now a mass of tumbledown homes and untended fields overrun by blackberries," Mann wrote. "Scattered among the houses and fields were skeletons bleached by the sun." Patuxet was especially hard hit; along the coast, not a survivor remained, though he and his party later encountered some inland. They sent for Massasoit, who had once ruled a community of several thousand people, and learned that only about sixty had lived. Taking over the settlement, the Pilgrims believed it was God's will that they had arrived on land already cleared and prepared for their presence.

Meanwhile, the first European settlers of the area that would become known as Dorchester set sail from England on March 20, 1630, on the ship Mary and John. There were 140 passengers aboard, primarily from the western counties of Devon, Dorset, and Somerset. The Puritans, as they were known, believed that the Church of England had not sufficiently purged itself of Roman Catholic practices after the Protestant Reformation of the sixteenth century and looked to practice their interpretation of Protestantism in the New World. After sighting the Massachusetts coastline in May, they changed their initial plan of landing at the mouth of the Charles River and headed instead to Nantasket Point, and from there to the mouth of the Neponset River. The natives there, the Neponsets—part of the larger Massachusett tribe—had been trading with Europeans since John Smith landed at the mouth of the river in 1614 and David Thompson established a trading post for furs in 1626 on the island in Boston Harbor that is today named after him.

A month later, in June, a much larger fleet of eleven ships carrying a thousand settlers from the Massachusetts Bay Company arrived in New England, led by John Winthrop. After landing briefly in Salem, where they considered the ground too stony for settling, Winthrop took the company further south to a neck of land between the Charles and the Mystic Rivers called Charlestown, where a small British settlement had been founded a year earlier. But when several members of his party fell ill, and the cause was attributed to bad well water, Winthrop chose to move the group across the Charles, to a small peninsula known as Shawmut where one colonist, the Reverend William Blaxton, had made a home on the western slope of Beacon Hill. Blaxton assured Winthrop that the pure spring water on Beacon Hill was sufficient to support his band of Puritans. The group built houses on the hills around the harbor and overlooking Back Bay, including Fort Hill, Beacon Hill, Pemberton Hill, and Copp's Hill in what later became the North End. They named their settlement "Boston," after the town on England's east coast that was the home of several prominent colonists. A few years later, in 1634, Braxton's farm became Boston Common, a plot of pasture land in the center of the settlement where the colonists could graze their livestock.

The settlers along the Neponset erected tents and cabins in an area they called Dorchester, after one of the towns in England's southwestern counties that many of them had called home; the natives referred to the area as Mattapan. The first area settled was near today's Edward Everett Square, where Columbia Road and Massachusetts Avenue meet. Its location along the shore and surrounding woodlands provided ample fish and timber, and the water power of the Neponset River enabled the settlers to establish the first grist mill in the United States.

"For the Indians, who called the area Shawmut, it was the treasure of the shellfish and the salmon, alewives, and herring that ran up the rivers each spring that drew them to the area," wrote historian Sam Bass Warner Jr. in "A Brief History of Boston," his chapter of the 1999 book *Mapping Boston*, edited by Alex Krieger and David Cobb with Amy Turner. "For the Europeans, the flood plain meadows gave grasses for their cattle, the valleys and gentle slopes afforded plow lands, and the gravel hills poured sweet water into their wells."

FIRST CONTACT

Between the two Puritan settlements struggling to survive in a new land was another, largely uninhabited peninsula. Known variously as Mattapan Neck, Mattapannock, Dorchester Neck, and Great Neck—and, ultimately, South Boston—this 560-acre patch of hills, orchards, and pastureland had never hosted a permanent human settlement. It was not reachable by land from the Shawmut Peninsula, or present-day Boston; it had to be crossed in canoes or other small craft. From Dorchester, the only way onto the neck was a causeway near present-day Dorchester Avenue at Andrew Square that often flooded in high tides or bad weather. In the summer months, natives would come to its mudflats, marshes, and shores to dig for clams or collect from its rich harvest of scallops, oysters, and fish. The three rivers that drained the area—the Mystic, the Charles, and the Neponset—were teeming with fish. But no human trace remained on the neck when the weather turned cold.

With the neck largely inaccessible to Boston, it was the Dorchester settlers who got there first. In 1635, another shipload of migrants arrived in Dorchester, led by the Reverend Richard Mather. Along with a hundred passengers and a crew of twenty-three came another twenty-three head of cattle, three calves, and eight mares. They were all pastured on Dorchester Neck, and a fence was erected across the causeway to keep the livestock from straying.

The first European to establish a home on Dorchester Neck was Captain Hopestill Foster, who owned a large lot known as Leek Hill, at the intersection of present-day Second and Dorchester Streets. But for the next century and a half, as Dorchester and Boston prospered, the farmers, fishermen, traders, and merchants of the two towns began to develop a lucrative cross-Atlantic shipping business that turned Boston into the second-largest British port in the world, after London. South Boston remained isolated pastureland and orchards, with no more than a dozen permanent inhabitants.

Just offshore, on Castle Island—which would not be connected to mainland South Boston until the twentieth century—Governor Thomas Dudley erected a small fortification in 1634 to help protect the harbor. That small garrison remained until the early 1700s, when British military engineers determined that the important port of Boston needed better protection and built a new fortress called Castle William on the island.

But on shore, the livestock continued to outnumber the humans, and South Boston was largely forgotten. It took a bold and somewhat desperate military commander, George Washington, to see the critical role South Boston could play in his efforts to drive the British army out of Boston—the first step in a long, unlikely rebellion that culminated in the overthrow of British rule and the founding of the United States.

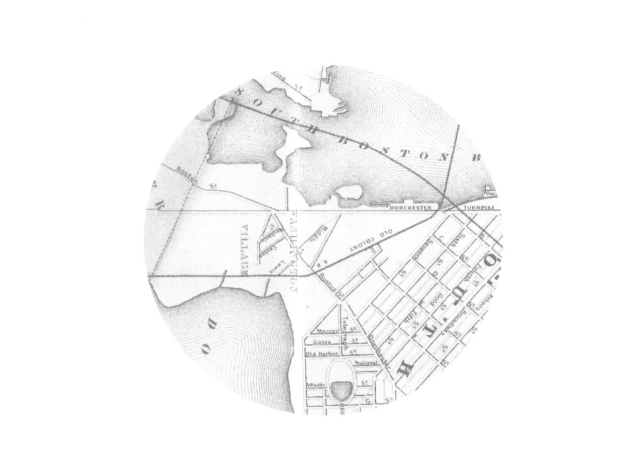

Chapter 2. Fortification and Evacuation

After the peace and prosperity of the first century of British settlement in North America, economic and political conditions turned sour in New England. Warfare among the European powers spread to the colonies at mid-century, first with King George's War from 1744 to 1748, then the French and Indian War, from 1754 to 1763. While King George's War was fought mostly on the North American frontiers—Acadia, or present-day Nova Scotia, Saratoga and other outposts in New York, and as far east as present-day North Adams, Massachusetts—the war exacted a heavy human toll. By some estimates, 8 percent of the adult male population of Massachusetts lost their lives in the fighting. When peace came, few of the underlying issues in North America were resolved, and borders between French and British territories remained undefined.

War broke out again in North America in 1754, and two years later in Europe. The French and Indian War, as it was known in the American colonies, was fought along the frontiers of British and French North America as the two superpowers battled for control of the continent. The British, with two million settlers in North America, vastly outnumbered the sixty thousand French colonists. Both sides enlisted Native Americans as allies. After major British victories across the northwest frontier of Canada in Ticonderoga, on the western shores of Lake Champlain, and at Fort Niagara, on the shores of Lake Ontario north of Niagara Falls, the British scored a major victory in defeating French forces on the Plains of Abraham in Quebec City in 1759. Ultimately, the French surrendered all of their territory in continental North America east of the Mississippi to the British, save for two small islands in the Gulf of St. Lawrence, in the Treaty of Paris that officially ended the war in 1763.

The victory earned Britain undisputed control of all of eastern North America, but it came at a severe cost. The wars in Europe and the Americas nearly doubled Britain's national debt, leading King George III and his ministers to determine that the colonies had a duty to help pay for their own defense. The resulting taxes imposed—first the Stamp Act of 1765, which levied a tax on all documents in North America, and, later, duties on items such as tea and sugar—infuriated the Americans. Until this point, the colonists had paid relatively little into the royal treasury, so the new taxes were an economic burden. Equally as troubling, however, was the idea that a government more than three thousand miles away could impose these charges unilaterally, with the colonists having no voice in the deliberations. "No taxation without representation" was a principle they could rally around. The new duties slowed the economy further and shifted activity away from major cities to smaller ports where the tariffs could more easily be avoided.

As opposition to the king's policies hardened, the stagnating port of Boston became a center of the resistance. Boston's Sons of Liberty protested the new duties on tea in November 1773 by boarding three cargo ships that had entered the harbor—the Dartmouth, the Eleanor, and the Beaver—and tossing chests of the imported tea overboard into the harbor. Britain responded forcefully, shutting down the port, revoking self-government in Massachusetts, and sending four thousand troops of British regulars to Boston to restore order.

Those troops were deployed into battle in 1775, first in April, when they were sent out to Concord to destroy stores of ammunition and supplies the colonial military leaders were stockpiling there. In June, fearing that British soldiers were preparing to occupy the strategic hillsides surrounding Boston, colonial military leaders sent 1,200 troops to occupy Breed's Hill and Bunker Hill in Charlestown, which protected Boston from the north. In re-

20

sponse, the British attacked on June 17, retaking the high ground but suffering casualties of 226 dead and 828 wounded (colonial losses were roughly half that). Despite the "victory," the British commander in Boston, General Thomas Gage, was dismissed from his post, replaced by General William Howe. Both sides hardened their positions, with the British determined to stamp out a rebellion and the colonists, newly organized after meeting in the Continental Congress in Philadelphia, sending a veteran of the French and Indian War, George Washington, to take command of the ragtag rebel forces.

Washington, forty-three, accepted the offer to lead the Continental Army on June 16, 1775. He had been nominated in the Continental Congress by Samuel and John Adams of Massachusetts in a show of unity. The congress chose Washington over the Bostonian John Hancock primarily because of his military experience; his Virginia background also served to demonstrate that colonial opposition to British policies in North America extended beyond the narrow confines of New England. Washington, proud, tall, strong, and erect, with pale skin and brown hair, arrived in Cambridge to assume command of his troops in early July.

Washington was taken by the verdant hills and rocky shoreline of New England in the summertime, describing it as "very delightful country." But his troops and supplies were in far worse shape than he had been led to believe. The "continental" army was composed almost entirely of New Englanders whose enlistments would be up at the end of the year, and they were fewer in number—fourteen thousand actually fit for duty—than the twenty thousand he had been told he would be leading. A proper Southerner, Washington's first impressions of New Englanders were not positive. He wrote to his cousin and business manager Lund Washington that Yankees were "exceedingly dirty and nasty," according to David McCullough's *1776*, a perceptive and well-researched examination of the events in the pivotal first year of the American Revolution. To another fellow Virginian, Congressman Richard Henry Lee, he wrote that he had contempt for "these people," who demonstrated "an unaccountable kind of stupidity in the lower classes."

Facing him across the Charles was William Howe, a member of Parliament and brother of Richard, Admiral Lord Howe, who had fought bravely in Quebec. He was roughly the same age as Washington at forty-five, but he had much more military experience, better troops, and several ships of the British Navy at his disposal.

When the dispiriting news of the results of the battle at Bunker Hill reached London in July, it further stiffened King George III's resolve to stamp out the rebellion in America once and for all. He sent two thousand reinforcements to Boston immediately, with plans to increase the army to twenty thousand by the spring of 1776.

Both generals shared a similar assessment of the conditions around Boston, and what it would take to break the stalemate. Boston proper was essentially confined to the Shawmut Peninsula, and the only access to it by land was across a narrow neck that roughly followed the route of present-day Washington Street. Washington and his forces easily could blockade the neck and prevent the overland movement of goods and people into Boston. The British Navy had control of the seas and the forts at the entrance to the harbor, so the troops could be resupplied.

The residents of Boston were another matter. Two-thirds of the population fled during the siege of Boston, with the British sending several boatloads of the town's poorer men, women, and children across Back Bay to rebel-controlled Cambridge, forcing the colonists to deal with about three hundred displaced refugees. To the north, despite the heavy losses incurred during the fighting, the British controlled Bunker and Breed's Hills in

Charlestown, assuring that their troops were safe from enemy fire in that direction.

The biggest prize for both armies lay to the south, on that windswept, nearly empty pastureland that was connected to Dorchester by another neck. The hills in South Boston, today known as Dorchester Heights, were, at an elevation of 112 feet, twice as tall as Bunker Hill; whoever commanded those heights, and could place cannon up there, was in easy range of firing on Boston and the ships in its harbor. Indeed, Howe's predecessor, Gage, had planned to seize the heights right after the Battle of Bunker Hill. The large losses the British suffered, along with Gage's dismissal, thwarted those plans. But the dozen or so families who lived on Dorchester Neck recognized the strategic importance of the heights, as well as the risk of relying on a single escape route that was often flooded and impassable. They quickly abandoned their homes.

Howe understood how vulnerable his position was if the Americans were to take the heights, but he had another idea on how best to succeed against the rebels—evacuate Boston entirely. He and his generals, along with military leaders back in London, were convinced that the British should withdraw to New York and launch attacks from there. He even received orders to that effect, to "abandon Boston before winter," from his superiors overseas. Unfortunately, by the time he received those orders, winter had set in.

Washington, meanwhile, vacillated in his preparations. His first thrust was to take the war to Canada, and surprise the British with an attack on Quebec. A thousand volunteers, led by Connecticut's Benedict Arnold, headed up the Kennebec River in Maine, an expedition that would end indecisively. While this was occurring, Washington plotted a direct attack on Boston, an amphibious landing with troops sent from Cambridge across the shallow Back Bay in flat-bottom boats, with fifty men in each one. He knew that such an attack would lead to terrific losses of life and the destruction of Boston, but he was also aware that winter was approaching and he had no barracks or firewood. Indeed, on January 1, with enlistments expiring, he likely would have no troops.

Over the summer and fall, both his own war council and a congressional committee of three, including Benjamin Franklin, agreed that an attack was not worth the total destruction of Boston. Once the committee rendered its decision in October of 1775, Washington had no choice but to order ten thousand cords of wood for fuel and begin building winter quarters for his men.

Just as both sides hunkered down for a long, cold, silent winter, Washington was intrigued by a seemingly outlandish proposal from one of his junior officers. Henry Knox, twenty-five, a self-educated bookseller who operated the London Book Store on Cornhill Street in Boston, had lost two fingers on his left hand in a hunting accident. Still, though, at six feet tall and 250 pounds, he wanted a military career. He met and fell in love with Lucy Flucker, the daughter of one of his bookstore's patrons, Thomas Flucker, who served as royal secretary for the province of Massachusetts. Though Thomas Flucker objected to Lucy's plans to marry Knox, Flucker arranged for Knox to be offered a commission in the British army. Knox refused and, after the Battle of Lexington and Concord, fled with Lucy to Worcester to join with the rebels. Lucy would never see her parents again.

Knox became intrigued with the story of the capture of Fort Ticonderoga in upstate New York by Ethan Allen, Benedict Arnold, and the Green Mountain Boys, which had occurred in May. Knox presented Washington with a bold proposal: He would lead an expedition to Fort Ticonderoga, retrieve the cannon and ammunition that had been seized there, and take them back to Massachusetts to be placed on Dorchester Heights.

FORTIFICATION AND EVACUATION

Washington approved the idea at once, and on November 16, 1775, along with his nineteen-year-old brother William, Knox set out for Lake Champlain. Traveling at a brisk pace of as much as forty miles a day, they reached Fort Ticonderoga in less than a month. There, they found a cache of weapons, mostly mortars and cannon that had been captured by the British from the French in 1759, during the French and Indian War. Knox selected fifty-eight of the best weapons to transport back to Boston. It wasn't easy; a twenty-four-pound cannon can weigh more than five thousand pounds. Altogether, according to McCullough, Knox's bounty weighed approximately 120,000 pounds.

He managed to sail the guns down Lake George before it froze over, then transported them by oxen-drawn sleds. Despite a few thaws along the way, the guns arrived in Framingham, twenty miles to the west of Washington's Cambridge headquarters. The course of the campaign was about to change dramatically.

With the ground frozen and the terrain steep around Dorchester Heights, digging trenches and throwing up fortifications during the winter was impossible. Washington chose to build the fortifications off-site, and then drag them up to the heights in secret along with the guns. To do that, a wall of hay bales had to be constructed along both sides of the causeway connecting Dorchester to South Boston—the area around present-day Dorchester Avenue in Andrew Square—to hide the activity from British view.

To accomplish all this work, three thousand men were enlisted to help fortify the heights, while an additional four thousand were positioned in Cambridge with flatboats at the ready to attack Boston once the British launched their expected assault on the new fortifications. An additional two thousand militia members were called up, as well as supplies such as wagons, carts, and oxen.

The manpower was available because, in the time since Knox had set out for Ticonderoga, morale among the American troops had shifted profoundly. On New Year's Day, 1776, the first copies of the speech King George III had given at the opening of Parliament that fall were received in Cambridge. The king had accused the rebels of professing loyalty while preparing for war. "They have raised troops, and are collecting a naval force. They have seized the public revenue, and assumed to themselves legislative, executive, and judicial powers, which they already exercise in the most arbitrary manner. ...And although many of these unhappy people may still retain their loyalty ... the torrent of violence has been strong enough to compel their acquiescence till a sufficient force shall appear to support them." "The rebellious war," he said, "is manifestly carried on for the purpose of establishing an empire." Reaction among the American troops was electric. As many as nine thousand of the men who were eligible to go home decided to stay.

Back in Boston, meanwhile, conditions were worsening. The British troops were not used to a harsh New England winter, and some on Bunker Hill froze to death while on watch. The Navy was having a harder time getting supplies into Boston, between increased plundering by American privateers and bad weather in the North Atlantic. Private homes, as well as Old North Church, were ripped up and their siding and framing were used for firewood. Just four thousand residents remained in the town—a quarter of the population of 1750—and conditions were growing worse as food stocks dwindled.

Washington chose General John Thomas of Marshfield to lead the fortification of Dorchester Heights. Thomas, fifty-two years old at the time, trained as a surgeon, volunteered for service in Nova Scotia during King George's War in 1746 and discovered a preference for military life over medicine. The operation was to start on Saturday, March 2, 1776, culminating in a com-

26

plete occupation of Dorchester Heights by the first light of dawn on Tuesday, March 5, the anniversary of the Boston Massacre.

Washington first placed some of the heavy cannon Knox had obtained from Ticonderoga in Cambridge and Roxbury. At midnight on March 2, those cannon commenced firing, creating a diversion for the British troops. The colonial cannon fired constantly from midnight to dawn both Saturday and Sunday nights, with the British artillery roaring in response. For all the sound and fury, there was little damage done, just as Washington intended.

The rebels resumed fire again Monday night, March 4, and this time Thomas used it as cover to begin moving his troops into position along the causeway connecting Dorchester to South Boston, which had been lined with hay bales on both sides to conceal military activity. After first sending an advance guard of eight hundred to make sure the British had not learned of his plans, Thomas sent the rest of the company across the neck and up to the heights, with hundreds of carts filled with hay bales, barrels, guns, and everything they needed to fortify their position. The weather, for once, cooperated; the night was mild and the moon was full.

In Cambridge, two of Washington's other generals marched four thousand troops on the Common, another diversionary show of force to distract the British. If their actions had lured the British away from their positions, those Cambridge troops were poised to launch their flat-bottom boats and move across Back Bay into Boston to engage the enemy. But the British stayed in place, and at around 3 a.m., another relief force of three thousand men marched along the silent, shrouded causeway to keep the work going, and scores of riflemen fanned out along the South Boston shores.

When the new day dawned, the British were completely taken aback by what the Americans had accomplished overnight. At least twenty cannon were in place, aimed at British forces on land and sea and easily able to reach them. "My God, these fellows have done more work in one night than I could make my army do in three months," Howe is said to have uttered in astonishment. He ordered a two-hour bombardment of the Americans' position on the heights, but the guns were unable to reach their targets.

Stunned, the British admiral in the port of Boston, Molyneux Shuldham, sent an urgent message to Howe that the British fleet would have to abandon the port if Washington remained in control of the heights; he could not leave his ships in such a vulnerable position. Howe ordered an immediate attack on South Boston, and transport vessels loaded with British troops began launching from Boston's Long Wharf, just across the harbor, at noon. But the weather turned sour by nightfall; first snow and sleet, then relentless rain. Howe called off the attack the next morning, March 6, and ordered the evacuation of Boston. A delegation of four representatives from Boston crossed the very same causeway that the American troops had used to such advantage under cover of a white flag; they carried an unsigned message, presumed to be from Howe, stating that he would withdraw his troops peacefully, without destroying Boston in his wake, if the Americans would allow his forces to go unharmed.

The following Sunday, March 10, some 1,100 Loyalists who had remained behind in Boston, mainly from the upper classes, boarded British ships and sailed just out of range of the Americans' cannon, where they stayed for a week, floating on the tides. Not until March 17 did the winds turn favorable and a force of eight thousand Redcoats marched onto their transports. All told, an armada of 120 ships, carrying eleven thousand people, evacuated—but not before one last show of imperial British might. The entire fleet anchored at King's Road (later patriotically renamed to President Roads), the main deepwater passage out of the harbor. There, they waited for General Howe's flagship, the Chatham, to pass, before they all fired twenty-one

FORTIFICATION AND EVACUATION

gun salutes—"an ear-splitting reminder of royal might," as McCullough described it—and eventually headed to Halifax, Nova Scotia.

That afternoon, the first contingent of five hundred troops from Roxbury marched into Boston to claim the city. Washington himself waited a day before inspecting the damage left behind, then returned to Cambridge before he and his army marched off to New York on Thursday, April 4.

Across the channel, Dorchester Neck also was evacuated almost as swiftly as it was occupied. With the armies gone, the fortifications were abandoned, and the hills and fields that produced the most spectacular and unexpected victory of the brewing rebellion reverted to peaceful pastures and orchards.

DORCHESTER HEIGHTS AT THE BEGINNING OF THE NINETEENTH CENTURY, LOOKING FROM BOSTON COMMON.

Dorchester Heights from Boston Common at the beginning of the nineteenth century. *Illustrated History of South Boston.*

29

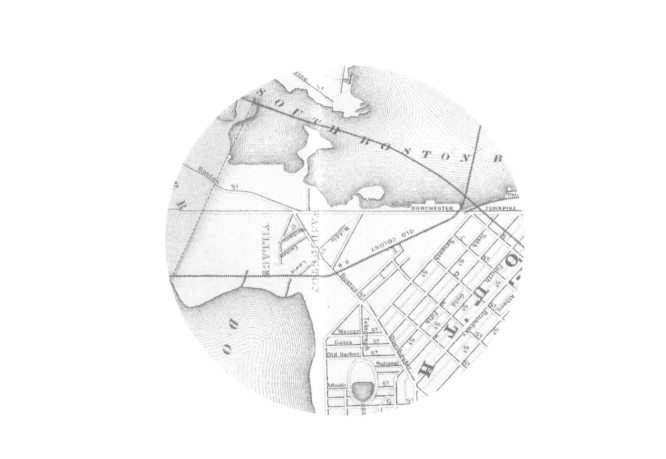

Chapter 3. Annexation and Expansion

Four decades of near-constant warfare brought hardship and economic stagnation to New England, and especially to Boston, which lost many of its well-to-do inhabitants and much of its trading might during Britain's blockade of the port and subsequent occupation and evacuation. All that changed with the signing of the Treaty of Paris in 1783, marking the official end of hostilities. The British public had always been split on warfare with the colonies; yes, the rebels defied the Crown, but their demands aroused much sympathy in the mother country. The peace negotiators gave the Americans full control of all British territory in North America from Florida north to Canada, and westward to the Mississippi River. More significantly for Boston, the treaty ended all economic restrictions on Britain's former colonies, allowing them to trade freely with the British Empire and anywhere else in the world.

By the end of the eighteenth century, Boston merchants had built lucrative trade relationships across Europe, the West Indies, South America, and all the way to China. Though New England had few of the raw goods that made for valuable exports, it could turn raw materials such as molasses, sugar, and hemp into valuable trading commodities such as rum and rope. The growth of trade spurred the development of other supporting industries, such as shipbuilding, insurance, and finance, to raise and protect the capital necessary for long and dangerous voyages.

Boston's newfound prosperity brought significant challenges to the tiny peninsula of just 750 acres. Its population, which had remained constant at about sixteen thousand for most of the eighteenth century before emptying out in the British evacuation, began to rise—the town counted eighteen thousand inhabitants in 1790, and twenty-five thousand people by the turn of the century. How could the town accommodate its growth?

31

From its inception, Boston was faced with two obvious ways to grow. The first was to build more land. Though it was isolated on a small peninsula connected to the rest of the region along a narrow neck, it was surrounded by tidal flats that were under water only intermittently. At low tide, vast expanses of salty marshes and mud flats were exposed. From the start, property owners along the shore were tempted—and, after 1641, allowed—to consider these flats as part of their property. That year, Massachusetts Bay Colony deemed that all of the shoreline down to the low-tide line, or one hundred rods (1,650 feet) from the high-tide line, should be considered as private property, contrary to European practices dating back to Roman times. The colonial lawmakers sought to encourage shorefront property owners to build private wharves onto the flats to encourage shipping, but over the following centuries the law also cleared the way for wharf owners to fill the areas between wharves and create new land.

Boston's other option was to annex surrounding farmlands and settlements. Given the transportation limitations of the eighteenth century, when most business and social intercourse was conducted on foot or, for a limited few, on horseback, there were practical limits on how far from the city center residents could live. For the scattered few residents who tried to make a home on Dorchester Neck, the distance they needed to travel to attend schools or religious services at the meetinghouse in Dorchester was a problem. The

FIND OLD BOUNDARY STONE.

Dorchester-Boston Marker Unearthed

by Subway Diggers.

A granite stone nine feet high and two feet wide at the base, tapering to one foot at the top, believed to be a boundary stone of a century ago, was unearthed under Dorchester av yesterday by workmen making excavations for the third section of the Dorchester subway. On one face of the stone is the letter "D," which is supposed to have indicated Dorchester, and on the other side the letter "B," which probably indicated Boston.

Between 1804 and 1855 all the territory west of West 8th st, South Boston, was known as Dorchester, including what is now known as Washington Village, or the Andams-sq district. Prior to 1804 all east of Mattapannock, but In March of that year a legislative order set aside all that part of Mattapannock east of West 8th st as South Boston.

Boston Globe, July 8, 1815.

View from "The Bridge of Sighs," as it was popularly known, the first bridge connecting South Boston to downtown. "Amérique septentrionale état de Massachusetts: view of Boston and the South Boston Bridge." Print. 1820. Adam, Victor, Deroy, Laurent, and Jacques Gérard Milbert. *Digital Commonwealth.*

distance was made worse by the unpredictable conditions along the neck around present-day Andrew Square; floods, bad weather, and high tides often made the road impassable. The causeway was a source "of vexation to the dwellers at the Neck, for at high tide, it was rendered impassable," wrote Charles Bancroft Gillespie in his *Illustrated History of South Boston* in 1900. "When this happened on Sundays, it interfered with the good intentions of those who desire to 'attend meeting.'"

But for Boston, the open fields and pastures of Dorchester Neck were tantalizingly close, if they could be made accessible by bridge. A group of Boston real estate developers known as the Mount Vernon Proprietors purchased large swaths of land on Dorchester Neck in 1803. The proprietors, who had helped lay out and build Beacon Hill, included well-known town residents such as William Tudor, William Gardiner, William Green, Jonathan Mason, and Harrison Gray Otis, one of the wealthiest men in Boston who later served as a United States senator from Massachusetts.

Almost immediately, land prices on Dorchester Neck rose tenfold, and Boston petitioned the legislature to annex the area from Dorchester. Dorchester residents resisted, but having done little to change conditions on the neck for a century and a half, they lost the debate; Boston gained control and renamed the area South Boston. With the addition of South Boston's 579 acres, the town nearly doubled in size with the stroke of a pen.

The same piece of legislation also authorized construction of a private toll bridge between Boston and South Boston along roughly the same lines as the present-day West Fourth Street Bridge. That 1,551-foot bridge, variously known as the Boston South Bridge, the South Boston Bridge, and later the Dover Street Bridge (as East Berkeley Street was formerly named), was popularly known as the "Bridge of Sighs" because courting couples often would meet on the bridge. Its location was not the first choice of the proprietors. The site was considered too far from Boston's commercial hub of Long Wharf to be of great use. However, wharf owners in South

Boston Globe, November 20, 1900.

34

Bay, which was then a body of water similar to Back Bay (stretching from today's Fort Point Channel to the South Bay shopping center), feared that a bridge built in a more central location would block access to their wharves and destroy their business. Their arguments won the day, and one year and $56,000 later, the bridge was opened for business. In the following year, 1805, the unpredictable, flood-prone causeway connecting Dorchester and South Boston was rebuilt as another private toll road, the Dorchester and Milton Turnpike. A toll gate was constructed at the junction of Boston Street (a section now called Dorchester Street), Preble Street, and the turnpike, which follows the route of present-day Dorchester Avenue.

In just two short years, the transportation infrastructure that has guided the development of the neighborhood for the next two centuries was essentially put in place. To the north, the previously remote Dorchester Neck was now part of Boston, connected to the town with a bridge that would quickly prove inadequate to the needs of a growing region. To the south, a major throughway provided fast, reliable access to the new neighborhood of South Boston and to the wharves and warehouses of Boston's waterfront that sat a short distance across the channel.

The New School at Washington Village.—Mr. Allen of Ward XII. renewed his motion to proceed to the election of head-master of the new school at Washington Village.

The two candidates were Mr. Leander Waterman, for four years, sub-master, and Mr. John Jameson, master, for fourteen years, of the Boylston school, which has recently been disestablished. All agreed that both gentlemen were excellent teachers, and the only question was, as stated by Mr. Fitzgerald, whether Mr. Waterman, who had for two years been practically filling the position of master, though having neither the title nor the salary of the office, should be displaced to make room for Mr. Jameson, or Mr. Jameson, who has taught for so many years in Boston, should, now that the Boylston school is disestablished, be thrown out of the city's employ. Messrs. Lane, Baldwin, Means, Johnson of Ward IV, and Richardson spoke in favor of Mr. Jameson's election, and Messrs. Allen, Fitzgerald and Underwood in favor of Mr. Waterman's.

After a discussion which lasted nearly an hour, Mr. Prescott moved the previous question which was ordered. The result of this ballot was as follows:

Whole number of votes..........59
Necessary for choice..........30
  Leander Waterman..........35
  John Jameson..........23

There was no election, and Mr. Adams of Ward XII. moved to take another ballot.

After further remarks from Messrs. Connor, Lane, Underwood, Adams of Ward XII, and Merrill of Ward XIV, Mr. Foster of Ward VIII, moved the previous question, which was ordered. The result of this ballot was as follows:

Whole number of votes..........60
Necessary for choice..........50
  Leander Waterman..........43
  John Jameson..........17

Mr. Adams of Ward XII. moved to again proceed

Boston Globe, July 16, 1873.

Though the Mount Vernon Proprietors laid out comprehensive plans for the buildout of South Boston, development proceeded slowly. As early as 1805, the major thoroughfares of Dorchester Street and Broadway were marked out, as well as the numbered streets (parallel to Broadway) and the lettered streets (perpendicular to Broadway) that still exist today.

Some of the initial wave of Irish immigrants who settled in Boston in the eighteenth century were among the first to populate South Boston, crossing the channel by bridge or rowboat to get to their jobs, or finding work on the South Boston side at some of the manufacturing and heavy industry sites that began to be located there. The slow pace of residential growth in South Boston led the town leaders to eye the neighborhood as a site for the large institutions that were outgrowing cramped quarters in Boston proper and needed to be pushed to the fringes of the town. Boston closed its almshouse for the poor in the West End in the 1820s and moved the residents to a fifty-three-acre piece of land near South Boston's City Point that included a House of Industry to put the poor to work, a House of Correction, and an Institution for the Reformation of Juvenile Offenders. A decade later, the Insane Hospital for the mentally ill was added to the complex.

The relatively remote location of the tolled South Boston Bridge hampered growth and led to near-constant political agitation for a second crossing nearer to Boston's waterfront. Opponents sometimes resorted to violence to fight to preserve the jobs they believed would be threatened by a new bridge. In 1811, seventy men armed with crowbars and maces smashed up one hundred feet of wharves under construction in the channel leading into South Bay; the wharves were viewed as a first step toward a new bridge in the area near Federal Street in Boston.

Boston, in need of land to house and employ its burgeoning population, first turned away from South Boston and toward the flats of the South End, creating twelve acres of new land between present-day Washington Street and Harrison Avenue. But Boston added another twenty thousand residents between 1800 and 1820 for a total population of more than forty-three thousand. By 1822 it had outgrown the town meeting form of government and reorganized itself into a city, with a mayor, a board of aldermen elected at large, and a common council with representatives from each ward.

Two years later, Mayor Josiah Quincy renewed the call for a new, free bridge to South Boston with a more direct connection to the waterfront, and he observed that "all the bitter animosities and apprehensions were renewed." But this time the legislature agreed, and by 1828, a new, free bridge was operating to connect the Dorchester Turnpike (today's Dorchester Avenue) to what was then called Sea Street but is now just an extension of Dorchester Avenue, in front of the Gillette Co.'s World Shaving Headquarters. All of the predictions made about the bridge turned out to be accurate. It provided the jolt desired to spur construction of commercial, industrial, and residential development in South Boston. But it also turned South Bay into the harbor's backwater, rendering many of the wharves in the brackish, sluggish tidewater economically useless.

DEDICATION.—The Lincoln Guard, Co. K, First Regiment, having fitted up a new armory in Washington Village, they last evening dedicated the same by a grand military and civic ball, which was attended by about one hundred and fifty couples, and was a very enjoyable affair. The number of military visitors was quite large, and included Brig.-Gen. Burrell and Major Bolster, of the First Brigade, Lieut.-Col. Choate, Major McDonough, Major Follett, of the Artillery Battalion, Major Blasland, and many others. During the evening the Armory Committee of the City Government were present, and expressed themselves as highly pleased with the condition of the armory. The ball was kept up to an early hour this morning.

Boston Post, February 19, 1874.

37

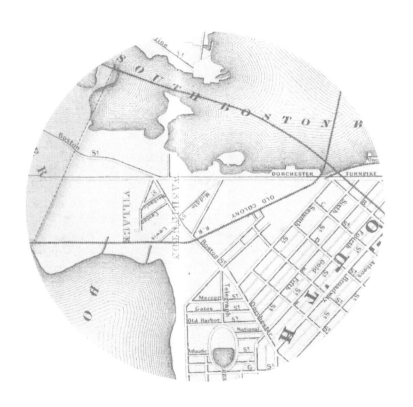

Chapter 4. Foundries, Factories, and Railroads

Flat, muddy, vacant, and flood-prone, the section of South Boston between the newly improved Dorchester Turnpike—today's Dorchester Avenue—and the shallow waters of South Bay offered few enticements for settlement. With the construction of the second bridge into Boston, South Bay's limited opportunity to develop a waterfront economy shriveled. Like Boston and the rest of New England, it possessed few natural resources that the rest of the country or, indeed, the world, wanted. But then, as now, Boston was home to an abundance of innovators and entrepreneurs who would produce goods and processes that would reshape the world over the course of the next century.

Cyrus Alger. *A Genealogical History of That Branch of the Alger Family Which Springs from Thomas Alger of Taunton and Bridgewater, in Massachusetts, 1665-1875.*

39

WASHINGTON VILLAGE: A SOUTH BOSTON NEIGHBORHOOD REDISCOVERED

In the early 1800s, the pioneers moving into the newly annexed territory of South Boston were manufacturers and heavy industry. Glass works, brass foundries, and iron foundries were soon scattered around the edges of South Boston, some employing as many as three hundred workers.

Along the shores of South Bay, the greatest and most influential of the iron foundries would arise. By the time of the Civil War, Cyrus Alger's South Boston Iron Co., known informally as "Alger's Furnace," was the largest foundry in the United States and a critical producer of cannon and ammunition for the Northern army.

Alger was born in Bridgewater, Massachusetts, in 1781, the second of six children. He first came to South Boston at the age of twenty-eight after learning the foundry business from his father, Abiezer, in nearby Easton. According to a family history, *A Genealogical History of the Alger Family Which Springs From Thomas Alger of Taunton and West Bridgewater,*

ALGER'S IRON FOUNDRY IN 1854.

An exterior view of Cyrus Alger's iron foundry in 1854. *Illustrated History of South Boston.*

INTERIOR OF ALGER'S IRON FOUNDRY IN 1850.

CASTING 25,000 POUND CANNON.

An interior view of Cyrus Alger's iron foundry as it cast a 25,000-pound cannon. 1850. *Illustrated History of South Boston.*

Massachusetts, 1665–1875, as a young man Alger was "a noted horseman and gunner, and in athletic exercises excelled all the young men in that section of the country."

He started a small foundry with a partner on Second Street in South Boston, then purchased a large swath of land between South Bay and the Dorchester Turnpike (today's Dorchester Avenue) to expand his business, incorporating in 1827. According to the family history, he bought the land between Dorchester Avenue and South Bay in 1816, making sure that the boundary stretched to the low-water mark in the bay. His descendant, Arthur M. Alger, wrote in the history that "the speculation was a bold one, and he was laughed at for his presumption in buying such a parcel of land for the purpose, as he avowed, of making building lots." But it helped cement Alger's fortune. Today, a small street off Dorchester Avenue named Alger Street marks the location of the second foundry.

SOUTH BOSTON.

The first concert of the Boylston Society of Washington Village, at its headquarters last evening, was attended by a large number of members and friends.

The Boylston orchestra played most acceptably. "The Merry Chanter," was sung by George Richardson and loudly applauded. The Sherwood quartet received deserved recognition from the audience. "Col. Wood's Grand March" was played on the piano by Fred Hunt. "The Schooner Hesperus," was sung by a large chorus of female voices. Banjos and mandolins were played finely by Messrs. Park, Davis, Lanton, Howes, Austin, West, Greene, and the trombone solo by I. B. M. Eliott was also very good. A cornet solo by William Mason, and song, "Easter Lillies," by Miss Bianch Newton, concluded a concert that was thoroughly enjoyable in every respect.

A bon bon party was given in Gray's Hall last evening, under the management of "Us Four," and was attended by about 200 couples.

The floor committee was in charge of C. H. G. Ferguson assisted by J. J. Cook, Miss Ella Anderson and V. F. Mitchell.

The final "show," of the Peoples' Entertainment Society in Dahlgren Hall, on E street, last evening, was attended by about 100 persons who were well pleased.

The new kindergarten in the Thomas N. Hart school, after one month in operation a week, has the full complement of pupil, 50. Other applications have been made, but as all the seats are occupied no more can be taken.

The parents of the children are much pleased with the innovation.

The driver of one of A. M. Stetson's coal teams fell off his seat near Silver street, last evening. He was taken into Alexander's drug store, and thence home.

An original entertainment will be held in Unity chapel this evening.

A new lodge of the Cadets of Temperance is being formed in this district.

Charles K. Dresser, about 30 years old, and residing in Washington Village, was thrown from his carriage on East 8th street this morning, slightly injuring his ankle.

The Rovers, a new social club, was organized last evening and elected the following officers: President, L. F. McCusick; vice-president, J. E. Foley; treasurer, W. R. Downey; recording secretary, F. J. Whitney; financial secretary, George Fox; craft; directors, Messrs. F. D. Hines, C. R. Haggerty and C. J. Ryan.

John H. Hudson was brought into court this morning by Officer Clough charged with embezzling one horse valued at $35, the property of one Charles S. Blood.

The case was continued until tomorrow. Hudson being held in $100. The case of L. Denihey, charged with using profane language on the street was continued until tomorrow, and he was held in $50 for his appearance.

Among the guests invited are Mayor Hart, Senator M. J. Creed, Aldermen E. J. Leary and T. W. Flood, Representatives J. L. McNamara, W. S. McNary, M. J. Moore, J. J. Lynch and Councilmen Casey and Blaney. A banquet and entertainment will be followed by dancing.

The annual exhibition of the South Boston art club will be opened in Bethesda Hall Monday evening, and will continue Tuesday and Wednesday evenings.

St. Augustine's Lyceum will observe its anniversary this evening in Bethesda Hall.

Boston Globe, June 12, 1893.

Alger was not the first to cast military equipment and ammunition out of iron, but he succeeded in creating a method of purifying cast iron that gave it more than triple the strength of his competitors, making the resulting items he created denser and more durable. He produced the first "rifled" gun in the United States in 1834, a process that cut grooves on the interior surface of a gun's barrel to cause the ammunition to spin and therefore to fly more accurately at its target. The largest cast-iron gun ever manufactured in America, the "Columbiad," was built at his foundry under Alger's personal supervision. He made the first bronze cannon ever cast for the United States government. The foundry supplied cannonballs for the War of 1812, and doubled its capacity after the Civil War broke out to supply the Union Army with guns, cannon, and ammunition. Alger's iron works, run by Alger's son Francis after Cyrus Alger's death in 1856, operated around the clock producing armaments during the war; Francis added a second foundry, a machine shop, and three new blast furnaces in 1863 to handle all the orders, according to Thomas H. O'Connor's *South Boston, My Hometown: The History of an Ethnic Neighborhood*. Its growth was so spectacular that by the 1850s, it had become the largest iron foundry in the country. Its production lines were by no means limited to weaponry; by the 1850s, according to Charitably Speaking, the newsletter of the Massachusetts Charitable Mechanics Association, "his establishment offered a daunting selection of products, ranging from Steam Engine Castings, Hydrostatic Presses, Large (to 1500 gallon) Kettles and Heavy Shafts, to Cast Iron Pipes, Cooking Ranges, Fly-Wheel Pulleys, Gratings, and iron frames for Chickering pianos." As late as 1885 the South Boston Iron Company continued to manufacture cannon and shells for the United States Navy.

Alger also was active in civic affairs, representing South Boston as an alderman in the mid-1820s. He was a strong proponent of the new South Boston bridge. He created land to expand his works by filling between wharves he owned in South Bay, and added to his land holdings by purchasing eleven acres of marsh south along the Dorchester Turnpike to attract other factories, building sidewalks and planting shade trees.

In his obituary, first printed in the *South Boston Mercury* in 1856 and later expanded upon in the book *History of South Boston,*

The First Annexations, If They May Be Called Such.

were in 1634, when Long, Spectacle, Deer and Hog islands were granted to Boston. In 1636 Noddle's island—East Boston—was placed under Boston's jurisdiction. This, perhaps, should be considered as the first important change in the territory of Boston, for by it the town gained 836 acres of land, which have become thickly settled and covered with important industries. It had but few families in 1636. South Boston, or Dorchester Neck, as it was called, with a population of about 60, was annexed in 1804. Washington Village, also a part of Dorchester, having a population of 1315, was annexed in 1855, making South Boston a district of 1002 acres. Thompson's island was granted to Boston in 1834. Roxbury, with a population of over 30,000, and having an area of 2760 acres, was annexed in 1867. Dorchester joined Boston in 1869, bringing about 12,000 people and 5814 acres of territory. In 1873 came West Roxbury, with about 9500 population and 7848 acres; Brighton, with over 5000 inhabitants, and 2277 acres, and Charlestown with about 30,000 people and 586 acres. All these annexations, with the area of the original town and the encroachments on the sea, give to Boston an area at the present time of 23,661 acres, or 36 7-10 square miles. The most recent computations of the city surveyor show slight variations in the areas of several localities from the preceding figures; these variations indicate that the total area of Boston is 23,890.8 acres, or 37 2-10 square miles.

Boston Globe, December 31, 1882.

formerly Dorchester Neck, now Ward XII. Of the City of Boston, by author Thomas C. Simonds, Alger was described as a benevolent owner who often kept his men employed at half pay when there was no work rather than lay them off, and he was the first employer in South Boston to introduce the ten-hour workday. "Mr. Alger's kindness to the men in his employ was proverbial," Simonds wrote.

Alger was not alone in finding ways to exploit and adapt the technological advancements of the nineteenth century to reshape the landscape of today's Washington Village into an industrial powerhouse. The first and most enduring transformative technology was the advent of the steam railroad in the 1830s. Prior to the coming of the railroads, navigable rivers and man-made canals were the major throughways of shipping and commerce inside the growing United States. Massachusetts and New England were largely devoid of, and located far from, major navigable rivers such as the Mississippi, the St. Lawrence, or the Hudson; without some form of large-scale improvements and investments, the port of Boston was in danger of losing business to New Orleans, New York, Montreal, Baltimore, and other major cities in eastern North America.

In the early part of the century, the need to move large quantities of goods from the farms, forests, fields, and factories inland to coastal ports kicked off a frenzy of canal building. The Erie Canal, connecting the Great Lakes to the Hudson River and New York, opened in 1825 and

---

Washington Village Yacht Club.

The clubs around Boston early opened some of their regattas to all yachts belonging to any recognized yacht club. A few of the residents and boat owners of South Boston and vicinity, wishing the enjoyment of these races, formed a small club at Washington Village, and called it the Washington Village Yacht Club. This was September 11, 1879. Its officers in 1883 were: Commodore, James G. Stewart; vice-commodore, I. B. Grose, Jr.; secretary, William E. Lincoln; treasurer, Joseph J. Bowers. It captain and treasurer, Joseph J. Bowers. It then had a membership of twenty, and four yachts. Nothing has been heard from this club since that time, and it is supposed to have gone out of existence.

Savin Hill Association.

FOUNDRIES, FACTORIES, AND RAILROADS

was an immediate success. The Chesapeake & Ohio Canal, first conceived by George Washington as a means of linking the Ohio River in Pittsburgh to the Chesapeake Bay, was begun a short time later but ran into serious construction and engineering obstacles along its path. In New England, the Blackstone Canal linking Providence, Rhode Island, to the farmlands surrounding Worcester opened in 1828 to great success; the Middlesex Canal, opened in 1802, eventually shipped the raw goods needed in the mills of Lowell and Lawrence up from the Charles River in Charlestown, and the finished products of the mills were barged back to the port of Boston.

In its time, the Middlesex Canal was viewed as a tremendous success. US Treasury Secretary Albert Gallatin called it "the greatest work of its kind that has been completed in the United States" in 1809. But its time, and the time of most canals, was short-lived. Railroads would soon prove to be a much faster and economical mode of transport; railroads could carry ten times the amount of cargo as canal barges, at a much faster speed, with less complex engineering hurdles. Entrepreneurs and investors in New England rushed in to claim the best routes and beat the competition to populous markets; as many as thirty independent railroads were operating through the region by 1865, fighting to win their share of freight and passengers.

The first three railroads to service Boston opened in 1835, according to Ronald Dale Karr's *The Rail Lines of Southern New England: A Handbook of Railroad His-*

Boston Globe, September 16, 1879.

tory, radiating out from the city and linking the port to other major population and commercial centers: the Boston & Lowell, the Boston & Worcester, and the Boston & Providence. They were followed a decade later by the Old Colony Railroad, chartered by the legislature in 1844 to operate trains over thirty-seven miles of tracks between Boston and Plymouth. The Old Colony began service the next year, in November 1845.

The Old Colony Railroad expanded aggressively to become one of the dominant transportation systems in the region in the nineteenth century, acquiring competing railroads and steamship companies. It immediately became a major presence in South Boston, carving its path southward along what is today known as Old Colony Avenue. It built a major Dorchester station at what became known as Harrison Square in 1844 to commemorate the visit of President William Henry Harrison to Dorchester in 1840. Today the neighborhood, cut off from the harbor by the Southeast Expressway, is known as Clam Point and is bounded by Beach Street, Freeport Street, Morrissey Boulevard, Victory Road, and the railroad and subway tracks on the inland side. Cyrus Alger himself sold part of the garden behind his house to the Old Colony, and the railroad developed its yards on the edges of

Boston Globe, March 17, 1890.

SOUTH BOSTON.

At a meeting of the Citizens' Association of Washington Village at the residence of James A. Kemp, the following officers and committees for the ensuing year were chosen: President, James A. Kemp; vice presidents, W. S. McNary, J. W. Tuttle and W. A. Gates; secretary, Walter Pritchett; treasurer, Edwin R. McLarin; committee on legislative affairs and local improvements, A. C. Richmond, William H. Horton, W. L. Lewis, W. H. Navary and the officers of the association. It was resolved to heartily indorse the Citizens' Association of South Boston and to co-operate with them in their endeavors to secure a playground in Washington Village and all other improvements beneficial. The committee on legislative and local improvement were authorized to ask the West End Street Railroad Company to improve the facilities on Dorchester street with cars for 10 minutes' transportation. There is a special committee of five on parkway from City Point to Franklin park, James A. Kemp, William H. Allen, Henry T. Bowers, Clarence E. Snow and George T. Wade. Committee on engine house, Washington Village, S. H. Tower, William H. Kemp and George R. Willis, C. R. Flynn, D. J. Cross, E. M. Sears, E. B. Wallace.

FOUNDRIES, FACTORIES, AND RAILROADS

Boston Globe, June 15, 1891.

ucts of Brockton's shoe factories and the textile mills of Taunton, New Bedford, and Fall River to the port, and passenger cars delivered travelers to the harbors of nearby Dorchester and far-off Plymouth and, ultimately, Cape Cod.

South Bay and the channel, site of today's present MBTA train and bus yards in South Boston.

Both the railroad's freight business and its passenger service were busy and profitable. Freight cars carried the finished prod-

The coming of the railroads also increased demand for the iron foundries and heavy equipment manufacturers that had clustered around Alger's South Boston Iron Company and the vacant mudflats he had slowly filled in stretching south between the Dorchester Turnpike and South Bay. The nearby Norway Iron Works, also on Dorchester Avenue, manufactured iron wire and sheet iron, operating nonstop six days a week. Fulton Iron Foundry, also in the neighborhood, and Bay State Iron Works at City Point employed thousands of workers; indeed, according to Gillespie's *Illustrated History of South Boston*, the neighborhood "boasted of the most extensive iron works in New England." One man and one company would rise above all others in its profound impact in reshaping and resculpting first Boston and then the American West: John Souther and his Globe Locomotive Works, manufacturer of the humble but revolutionary steam shovel.

Boston Globe, May 18, 1890.

Chapter 5. Reshaping the Landscape

Boston at midcentury was bursting at the seams. The potato blight that led to the Great Famine devastated Ireland, ultimately claiming more than a million lives and leading a million more to emigrate. Boston's population surged as a result; between 1840 and 1850 the US Census recorded an increase of more than forty thousand residents, to a total of 136,881. Of that total, 46 percent were foreign born. In 1847, the *Boston Transcript* described the city as full of indigent Irish immigrants, "groups of poor wretches ... resting their weary and emaciated limbs at the corners of the streets and in the doorways," according to author Stephen Puleo's 2011 book, *A City So Grand: The Rise of An American Metropolis, Boston, 1850–1900*. With much of the city's open land, and an abundance of unskilled jobs at its foundries and factories, South Boston also grew; the thirty-five residents who were counted in 1804 became about eighteen thousand by 1850, and thirty thousand by the end of the Civil War in 1865.

But Boston was not content with channeling all of its growth across to South Boston. The city was flattening out hills, filling in mudflats, and making new land in all directions. Today's South End began to be filled in during the 1830s, with the creation of Front Street (now Harrison Avenue) and Tremont Street. Much of the land that became the Public Garden, at the

Washington Village Park.

Councilman E. P. Barry of ward 15 offered an order requesting the mayor to petition the Legislature for permission to borrow $150,000 for a public park in Washington Village. Referred to the committee on finance.

Boston Globe, January 17, 1890.

edge of Beacon Hill and Boston Common, also was filled in during the 1830s. A dike and mill dam was built across the flats on the Charles River in today's Back Bay, in the hopes of generating power from the flow of the tides. That scheme never panned out, creating nothing more than a foul-smelling backwater that became further stagnant when two of the new railroads, the Boston & Providence and the Boston & Worcester, built their own embankments across the basin.

But those small attempts at city building were nothing compared to what was to come later in the century. Concerned about overcrowded conditions, poverty, sanitary shortcomings, and disease in the city's densely populated waterfront neighborhoods of Fort Hill and the North End, and worried that wealthier residents would take advantage of transportation advancements such as the railroad to abandon the city for surrounding towns, Boston embarked on an ambitious process to remake itself.

Over the course of the next five decades, Boston would embark on a building and expansion project in scale and size that makes the most ambitious project of modern times, the $15 billion Big Dig to depress the Central Artery and build a third tunnel to Boston Harbor, seem insignificant by comparison. The small 487-acre Shawmut Peninsula, home to twenty-five thousand inhabitants at the start of the century, more

FOR THE GOOD OF DORCHESTER.

Improvements Reported at Meeting of a Local Association.

A largely-attended meeting of the Washington Village Improvement Association was held last evening in Horton Hall, Dorchester av.

On motion of C. P. Flynn the question of the naming of the square in Washington Village was taken from the table and the name of Andrew square adopted by the association and referred to the City Council for its confirmation.

The committee on local improvements reported that at its request the superintendent of lamps has caused an electric light to be placed on Swett st. at the New York & New England railroad crossing, and would very soon place further lights on Swett st. as well as on Dorchester av.

The committee on travel and transportation reported that in an interview with the officials of the West End railroad that cor-

Boston Globe, May 18, 1891.

than doubled in size, as parts of the North End and South End were filled, the neighborhood of Fort Hill was razed and used to fill in the area that would become Atlantic Avenue, and the ambitious efforts to create an entire new upper-class enclave in the foul-smelling Back Bay basin added more than a hundred acres to the city.

These land-making projects, unprecedented in their scope, required one fundamental raw material: dirt. And that dirt had to be excavated from one location, transported to another, and spread there. John Souther and his company, Globe Locomotive Works, provided that muscle.

Souther, one of the greatest engineers, innovators, and industrialists the neighborhood ever produced, was born in South Boston on March 1, 1816. When he was fourteen, he became an apprentice carpenter and patternmaker for machinery, which led to a job in Cuba at age twenty-one as a draftsman and patternmaker for sugar-milling equipment. He returned to Boston two years later with the intent to manufacture machinery for Boston's sugar refiners, but instead connected with Holmes Hinkley, who

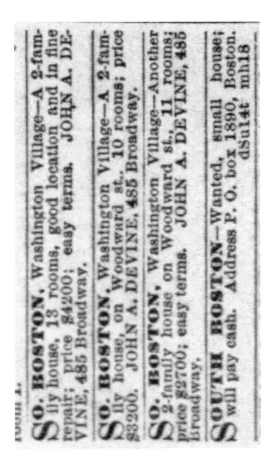

Boston Globe, March 22, 1892.

founded the Boston Machine Works across the channel and began building steam locomotives for the burgeoning railroad industry.

Five years later, in the early 1840s, Souther struck out on his own, building the first locomotive works in South Boston. His firm, Globe Locomotive Works, originally began at First and A Streets, roughly where the Gillette World Shaving Headquarters sits today along Fort Point Channel. But as his work expanded, he opened an additional factory adjacent to Cyrus Alger's complex at Foundry Street near the Dorchester Turnpike, and later still further south on Dorchester Avenue. Souther's locomotives were put in use by railroads all across North America. In 1849, he shipped one of his locomotives around Cape Horn at the southern tip of South America to California Territory, where it was put to use on the first railroad constructed between Sacramento and Folsom, the area of the Sierra Nevada foothills where the California Gold Rush began. Twenty years later, another of Souther's locomotives pulled Leland Stanford's private car to Promontory Point, Utah, where the Golden Spike was driven into a railroad tie to connect the Union Pacific and Central Pacific and create the first transcontinental railroad in the United States.

JOHN SOUTHER.

But Souther built much more than locomotives; in fact, by 1864, Globe Locomotive Works had changed its name to Globe Works Company and completely exited the locomotive business. Souther built the large boring machine

John Souther, founder of Globe Locomotive Works, who made possible many of the great construction projects of the late nineteenth century with his steam shovel and dredges. *Illustrated History of South Boston.*

Our Lady of Czestochowa, Boston Street, 1898. *Boston City Archives.*

563-573 Dorchester Avenue, 1898. *Boston City Archives.*

that was intended to tunnel through Hoosac Mountain in western Massachusetts to connect Massachusetts railroads to Albany and the West; that borer made it just twelve feet through the rock before failing in 1853. It would be another twenty years, and enormous sums of money for the time, before the approximately five-mile tunnel facetiously known as "The Great Bore" was complete, using hand-digging, blasting, and some of the first pneumatic drills.

It was the mechanical dredge that first steered Souther away from transportation and toward construction. Prior to 1847, dredging work in Boston Harbor was conducted by "chain bucket dredge" that could pull up soft mud but couldn't dig into harder, more difficult material. Souther's dredge, first put to use when South Bay was deepened and dug out to provide fill for the South End, consisted of a single scoop that could dig at the bottom, and a second machine that lifted up the dredged material and transported

492 Southampton Street, 1898. *Boston City Archives.*

493–501 Southampton Street, 1898. *Boston City Archives.*

it to the filled lands. Souther's improvements to the dredge allowed the work to be accomplished in one quarter of the time it previously took, according to Gillespie's *Illustrated History of South Boston*. Souther's dredging machines were subsequently used all over the world for the next half-century, including the Suez Canal in the Middle East and the Panama Canal in Central America.

But it was the steam shovel that sealed Souther's reputation for quality and innovation. He didn't invent the device; William Otis (cousin of Elisha Otis of elevator fame) created the first steam-powered mechanical excavator, in Canton, Massachusetts, in 1835, for a railroad company building a line to Worcester. Otis received a patent for a "Crane-Excavator for Excavating and Removing Earth" in 1839, but died that same year at age twenty-six.

Otis's cousin, Oliver Chapman, took over and continued tinkering with the excavator. In the 1850s, he contacted Souther about refining the machine to endure harsh, heavy construction conditions and reduce breakdowns. They worked on it throughout the 1850s, increasing its weight to ten tons so that it could dig through harder, denser materials. They put the "Chapman Steam Shovel" into production at the Globe Locomotive Works near the end of the decade, according to author Stephen Puleo.

Just at that moment, the City of Boston and the Commonwealth of Massachusetts were embarking on their unprecedented attempt to reshape the Back Bay's fouled, muddy wasteland into a posh neighborhood of wide boulevards, tree-lined residential streets, and stately town homes. Souther's new steam shovel, combined with his knowledge of railroads, af-

15-17 Ellery Street, 1898. *Boston City Archives.*

forded the perfect solution for moving, literally, mountains of dirt. He first dug into the hills of Newton and Needham for the fill he needed in the Back Bay, and when those were leveled off, he obtained gravel from Canton, Dedham, Hyde Park, and Westwood. According to the *Boston Daily Traveller*, which documented the Back Bay work in minute detail in 1859, a trainload of thirty-five cars could be loaded with gravel in Needham in about ten minutes; "the excavators do the work of two hundred men." As described in Nancy S. Seasholes's extensive documentation of the project in her book *Gaining Ground: A History of Landmaking in Boston*, the Back Bay received twenty-five shipments of gravel every twenty-four hours, with ten cars being emptied at a time, dumping the fill into huge mounds "from where it was then moved and leveled by horse-drawn scoops, scrapers,

39–41 Ellery Street, 1898. *Boston City Archives.*

and carts." The project was able to fill the equivalent of two house lots a day.

The Back Bay project, which proceeded methodically up along Commonwealth Avenue and Beacon Streets from the Public Garden to Kenmore Square, was ultimately so successful that authors Barbara Moore and Gail Weesner calculate that the state made a profit of $3.5 million from the project. And, of course, the Back Bay became exactly the wealthy enclave that was envisioned and drew a whole host of institutions to the neighborhood, from the Boston Public Library to Trinity Church to the Museum of Fine Arts and more.

7-9 Ellery Street, 1898. *Boston City Archives.*

RESHAPING THE LANDSCAPE

A hundred years before Boston's West End was razed and cleared in the name of urban renewal, Souther's steam shovels also cut down the fifty-four-foot high Fort Hill area of Boston, the city's first major attempt at slum clearance. Irish and other immigrants had crowded into homes on Fort Hill, located today roughly where the International Place towers are situated in the Financial District, just blocks from the waterfront. By some estimates, the three- to five-story homes on Fort Hill sometimes contained as many as a hundred inhabitants; such crowding was blamed for the cholera epidemic of 1849, which killed more than seven hundred Boston residents. The city successfully defended its right in court to take the land in 1866, then went to work to cut down the hill and use the materials and gravel to fill in along Atlantic Avenue to make a broad highway to businesses along the harbor, according to Seasholes.

Later in the century, Souther's technology also was put to use along the waterfront, dredging out Fort Point Channel, deepening the harbor, and filling in twenty-five acres of South Boston waterfront in the immense Commonwealth Flats project, another undertaking of the state to upgrade Boston's port facilities and create land for docks, warehouses, wharves, and future development around Commonwealth Pier (today's Seaport World Trade Center).

By the time of Souther's death in 1911, Boston was a city transformed. His locomotives had helped the city spread outward and connect the port and its jobs with goods and workers. His steam shovels and dredges had helped entire neighborhoods rise out of the muck and build the literal foundation of much of the city we know today.

Old Colony Avenue, 1912, Boston City Archives.

The First Annexations, If They May Be Called Such.

Boston Globe, Dec. 31, 1882.

THE PARK QUESTION.

Hearing on the Proposed Pleasure Ground in South Boston and Dorchester.

Boston Globe, Nov. 17, 1875.

Back Bay and South Bay Redeemed.

Boston Post, April 29, 1874.

SOUTH BOSTON.

Boston Globe, 1890.

383 Dorchester Ave. 1913, Boston City Archives.

AUCTIONS. REAL ESTATE
MORTGAGEE'S SALE OF REAL ESTATE

Boston Globe, 1915.

South Boston and Washington Village. The Large and Valuable Estate, Consisting of a 2½ Story Dwelling House and 13,350 Square Feet of Land, Corner of Dorchester and Vinton Sts.

Boston Globe, May 25, 1883.

South Boston, Peremptory Sale of 6 Valuable Building Lots, Corner Dorchester Av. and Dorchester St.

1874. Busch, Edward, Bourquin, F., and G.M. Hopkins & Co. "Map of the cities of Boston, Cambridge, Somerville and Chelsea, and the town of Brookline with parts of Newton, Malden and Everett." Detail. *Norman B. Leventhal Map & Education Center.*

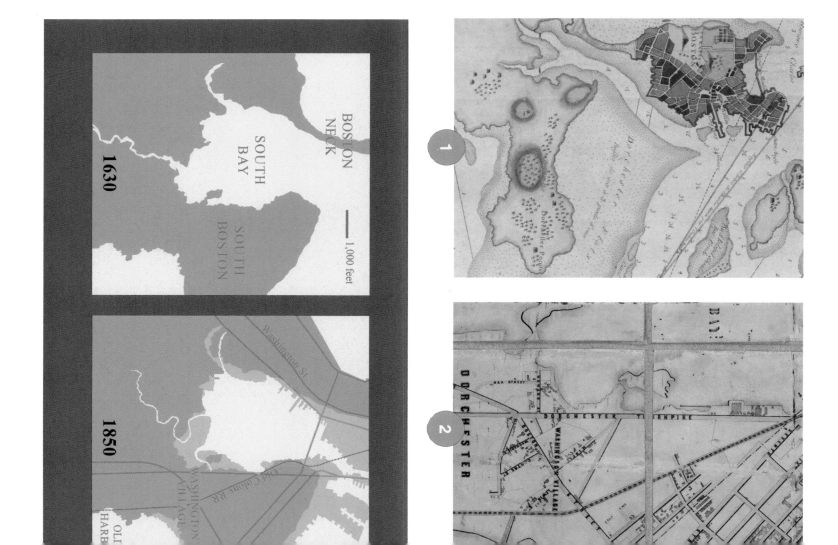

BOSTON
NECK

1630

SOUTH
BAY

SOUTH
BOSTON

——— 1,000 feet

1850

Washington St.

WASHINGTON
VILLAGE

Old Colony RR

OLD
HARBOR

BOSTON

Dorchester Flats

Dorchester Bay

1

DORCHESTER

OAK STREET

DORCHESTER TURNPIKE

WASHINGTON
VILLAGE

B D

2

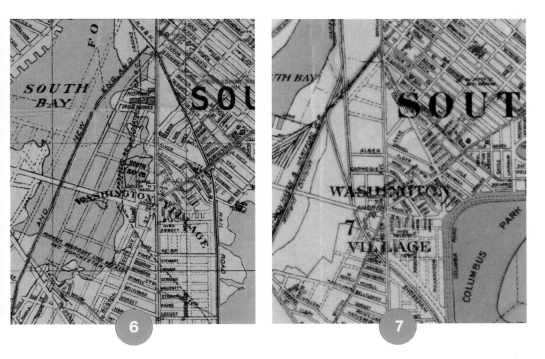

6. 1895. Geo. H. Walker & Co., International Society of Christian Endeavor, Estey Organ Company, and Estey Piano Co. "Official map of Boston." Detail.

7. 1927. Walker, George H. "Boston and surroundings." Detail.

Norman B. Leventhal Map & Education Center.

...Dorchester Neck also was evacuated almost as swiftly as it was occupied. With the armies gone, the fortifications were abandoned, and the hills and fields that produced the most spectacular and unexpected victory of the brewing rebellion reverted to peaceful pastures and orchards.

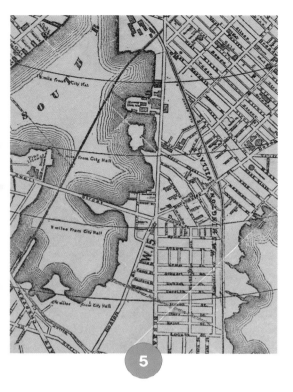

1. 1778. Le Rouge, George-Louis. "Plan de Boston avec les sondes et les directions pour la navigation." Detail.

2. 1852. McIntyre, Henry, et al. "Map of the City of Boston and Immediate Neighborhood." Detail.

3. 1859. Walling, Henry Francis, and F.A. Baker. "Map of Boston and Its Vicinity." Detail.

4. 1870. Davis, Thomas, W., and Boston Engineering Department. "Plan of Boston, with additions and corrections." Detail.

5. 1886. Schumm, Otto. "Map of Boston." Detail.

Norman B. Leventhal Map & Education Center.

5

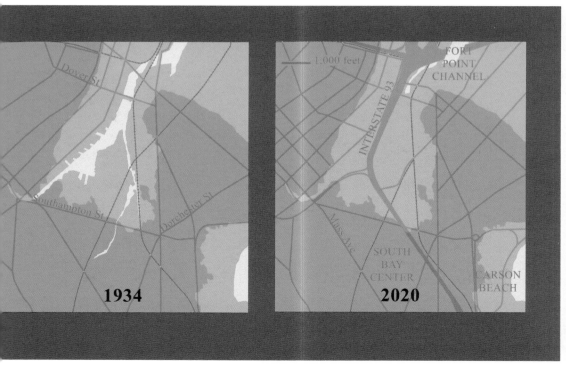

1934

2020

vid Butler, information from "Mapping Boston," Edited by Alex Krieger and David Hobb with Amy Turner.

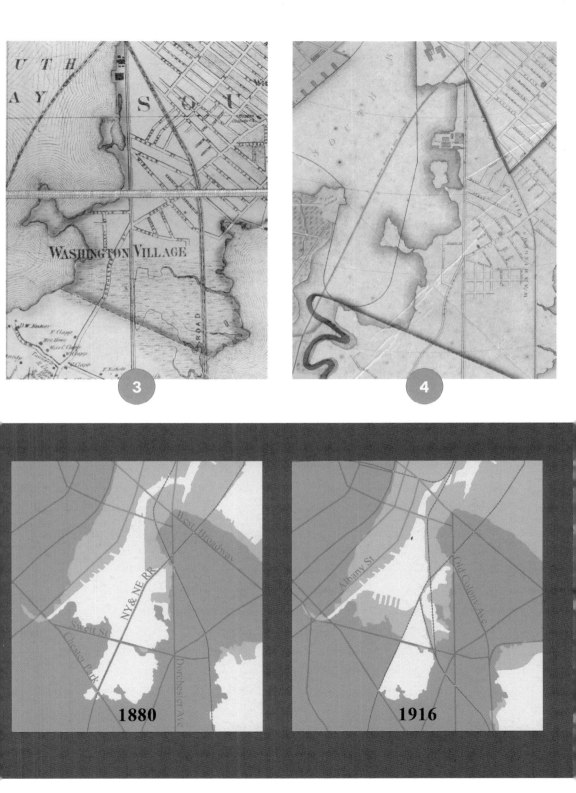

Washington Village area of Dorchester, then South Boston, as it evolved from 1630 to today. *Maps by D*

Leutze, Emanuel Gottlieb (1816-68). "George Washington at Dorchester Heights, Massachusetts" (color lithograph). *Private Collection / Peter Newark American Pictures, Bridgeman Images.*

CHANGES IN WASHINGTON VILLAGE.

New Location of Route of New York, New Haven & Hartford Road Affects Many Thoroughfares.

The topographical changes throughout Washington village, South Boston, are of a most interesting nature, and compare in importance with many other remarkable works now under way in different sections of Greater Boston. The new location of the route of the New York, New Haven & Hartford railroad has completely upset the map of this section of Boston and brought about radical changes in real estate lines throughout this vicinity.

By many old residents of the village it was thought that the neighborhood would be injuriously affected by the many changes already made, and those which are to come, as they were of the opinion that property values would suffer.

But quite a change in feeling has come over the people, as Boston st is now assuming an appearance of order, and there is now almost a general expression of approval at the improved condition of Boston st. The property along the line has been made to conform to the new grades, and the street with its new sidewalks and paving shows a graceful and clean-cut look.

It is assumed that the two other thoroughfares, Swett st and Dorchester av, will in like manner commend themselves to the favorable regard of the public when they are finished. Many buildings in this section are being reconstructed and repaired.

Saturday night a new line of electrics was opened over Boston st, where there is now a double track. The Dorchester av line and the South Boston line of transfer cars from Dorchester st, South Boston, to Field's Corner, are now using Boston st, Dorchester av having been closed to public traffic Saturday night. The grade of Boston st is now not at all as desirable to the bicyclist and teamster as heretofore. It has always been. . .

Boston Globe, Dec. 18, 1899.

SOUTH BOSTON WARDS.—It is understood that the City Committee on the Re-division of Wards have agreed that South Boston, east of Fore Point channel, and including Washington Village, shall have three wards. The boundaries will be as follows: Commencing at D street at South Bay, thence running through D street to Fourth street; thence through Fourth street to E street; and through E street to the Harbor Commissioners' line. Also commencing at the corner of Broadway and E streets, thence through the centre of Broadway to Dorchester street, thence through Dorchester street to Fourth street, to Atlantic street through to the Commissioners' line on Dorchester bay. Also the old boundary line between Dorchester and Washington Village. Thus it will be seen that all that portion of the peninsular lying west of D to Fourth streets, and west of E to First streets, and east of Fore Point channel will constitute one ward, and all the territory east of D, Dorchester

and Atlantic streets, and north of Broadway from E to Dorchester, and Fourth from Dorchester and Atlantic streets will be another ward, and the remaining territory will be a third ward.

Boston Post, August 23, 1875.

On Friday, in the Senate, the bill to incorporate the Bank of Mutual Redemption in Boston, was passed to a third reading. The death of Mr. Charles R. Webster, member of the House for Chelsea, was announced, and both branches adjourned to an early hour.

On Saturday, a bill was reported in the Senate to set off Washington Village from Dorchester, and annex it to Boston. It was read, and ordered to a third reading. The resolve appropriating $41,584.05 for the payment of expenses of criminal prosecutions in Suffolk County, occasioned considerable debate, and was refused engrossment. The House refused to take from table the motion to reconsider the vote whereby the bill loaning the credit of the State to the Vermont and Massachusetts Railroad was lost. The bill relating to the militia, (substituting an armed police system for our present militia force, except in the city of Boston,) after a warm

Boston Globe, May 12, 1855.

Yesterday was "flower Sunday" in many of the churches in this district. At St John's M. E. church, Rev W. T. Perrin, preached to boys and girls at the morning service. A fine concert, concluding with the distribution of plants to the members of the Sunday school, was held in the evening. Rev F. H. Hinman preached to the children of the Fourth Presbyterian church, and the Sunday school, under the direction of Mr James de Voy, gave a concert in the evening. The sermon for children in the Washington Village M E church was preached in the morning by the pastor, Rev A. H. Nazarian, his subject being "Little but Exceeding Wise," and in the evening a concert was held. In the Hawes Unitarian church the pastor, Rev James Huxtable, preached the sermon and the Sunday school exercises were held in the afternoon at 4 o'clock. The distribution of flowers to the scholars was the feature of the afternoon's exercises.

The funeral of Mrs Mary G., wife of patrolman Michael J. Cronin, will be held this morning at St Augustine's church at 10 o'clock. A committee of three fellow patrolmen has secured a handsome floral tribute.

The regular monthly meeting of the Washington Village improvement association will be held this evening in Harrison hall. It is expected some action will be taken on the decision of the fire commissioners as regards the placing of the new company in the new fire house.

At the annual meeting of the D. S. and L. A. yesterday afternoon the following officers were elected for six months: Miss Mary Manning pres, Mr Walter Butler vice pres, Mr Andrew Turnbull rec sec. Miss

Boston Globe, June 12, 1883.

IN WASHINGTON VILLAGE.

Progress of the Davitt Branch—A Largely-Attended Meeting.

The Davitt branch of the Irish Land League, which is located in Washington Village, had a largely-attended meeting in the rooms of St. Augustine's Lyceum last night. Mr. Michael H. Keenan, the president, occupied the chair, and Mr. James Riley, one of the vice-presidents, delivered a lengthy and carefully prepared review of the Irish agitation. The funds of the branch were increased by $22, and the membership roll had fifty new names added to it, which makes the present membership of the branch about 115. The following resolutions were presented by Mr. Keenan and adopted:

Whereas, we ask a beacon for our kindred who linger in the depths of misery and oppression, and whereas such a beacon will only shine on the hill tops of a happy and prosperous Ireland; therefore be it

Resolved, That we can never lay down our arms or cease our exertions until that prosperity is an accomplished fact, happen what may in the execution of such a project.

Whereas, the shackles of tyranny have bound the father of our branch;

Resolved, That we shall do all we can to unbar the prison door which confines the brave, true patriot, Michael Davitt.

Resolved, That our hearty sympathy is extended to his colleague, and that our devotion to the great cause and the great agitator will never cease until the objects of both meet with supreme consummation.

Boston Globe, March 3, 1881.

Auction Sales.

BY R. VOSE, JR., & CO.,
Auctioneers.

Office, 122 Washington street, opposite Water street, Boston.

LARGE SALE
—OF—
BUILDING LOTS,
NEAR WASHINGTON VILLAGE,
SOUTH BOSTON,
BY AUCTION.

WEDNESDAY, May 20, 1874, at 3 o'clock P. M.,
Will be sold, Fifty Lots of Land, containing from 1200 to 2000 feet each. These lots are situated near **Washington Village, on Dorchester Avenue, Boston Street, Blake Street and Washburn Street.**

☞ For particulars, inquire of GEORGE KEMPTON, Esq., 89 Washington street.

Boston Globe, May 20, 1874.

The Story of the Crime.

The crime of which Pomeroy was convicted was the murder of Horace H. Millen, aged 4 years and 3 months. It took place on that part of the marsh known as the "Cowpasture," which is between Washington Village and Savin Hill, in Dorchester.

The small boy lived with his mother in South Boston, and on the day of his death his mother had given him a penny to spend at a store near by.

Later in the forenoon he was seen with other small children and with an older boy, who was afterwards identified in court as Pomeroy by a young woman. Another woman testified that late in the day she saw the Millen boy and an older boy walking toward Washington Village.

Testimony of men and boys who were digging clams and saw the boys there, was that Pomeroy was leading his companion by the hand and helping him across a small creek.

Another witness testified to seeing a boy running away from the spot where the dead and mutilated body was found. The testimony was that the boy kept looking back as if fearing pursuit.

The convincing evidence against Pomeroy at the trial included the pocketknife in his possession with stains of blood and mud upon it, his plush cap, such as had been testified of by those witnesses who saw Millen and his older companion, shoe prints of his and of the Millen boy's on the beach, etc.

Pomeroy, when taken to the undertaker's rooms, would not look at the body of Millen, but when asked if he

Boston Globe, August 16, 1914.

409-411 Dorchester Avenue, 1917, *Boston City Archives*.

Chapter 6. Spreading Outward

Digging, dredging, and filling was just one method Boston used to expand its size, power, and influence in the second half of the nineteenth century. In addition to making new land on its historic original peninsula, Boston continued to cast its acquisitive eye at its neighbors. As it had first done in 1804 when it annexed South Boston, it again looked outside its borders for new ways to grow.

Like Boston, Dorchester also was transformed in the first half of the nineteenth century. The orchards, farmlands, and fields that had been home to about 2,300 people in 1800 had swelled almost four times in population, to eight thousand. The bridges constructed to connect Boston to South Boston wrought major changes in Dorchester, making the Dorchester Turnpike (now Dorchester Avenue) and the Old Colony Railroad (now Old Colony Avenue) major transportation corridors, along with other railroad lines along South Bay.

Around today's Andrew Square, a small settlement called Little Neck had developed, along the route that Washington's soldiers had taken to stealthily fortify Dorchester Heights during the American Revolution. The settlement, with homes clustered around railroad depots, had more in common with the urbanized, industrial corridor of South Boston than with rural Dorchester. Dorchester tried to help, building a brick schoolhouse for the residents, which by midcentury had grown to 1,300. Honoring its association to the events of 1776, the neighborhood renamed itself Washington Village in 1850 and petitioned multiple times to be separated from Dorchester and annexed to South Boston, according to Simonds's *History of South Boston*. Finally, in 1855, the petition succeeded.

Washington Village, as it turned out, was just the tip of the iceberg of expansion Boston would undertake in the second half of the nineteenth cen-

tury. In addition to its efforts to fill in around the edges of Shawmut Peninsula and expand its territory, Boston was investing major sums of money in
sewage and water systems and other public infrastructure. According to
Sam Bass Warner Jr.'s *Streetcar Suburbs: The Process of Growth in Boston
(1870–1900),* fully "one third to one half of the City's of Boston's budget was
annually committed to projects and services directly affecting real estate";
indeed, the city's annual spending was routinely larger than the budget of
the state of Massachusetts.

For Boston, the investments were the key to enticing neighboring communities to become part of the city. In return for acquiring land to house the

Boston Globe, September 20, 1899.

continued influx of immigrants, expansion to the suburbs would allow Boston to retain the wealthy taxpayers who had taken advantage of the coming of the railroads to move out of the city and acquire more land. For the surrounding communities, annexation to Boston solved the thorny questions of how to provide the level of services to their residents that Boston was providing.

Roxbury was the first, approving annexation by a wide margin in 1867, adding its 2,100 acres of land and 30,000 residents to Boston. Dorchester followed in 1869; though the vote there was more contentious, it narrowly passed, and Boston voters approved by a six-to-one margin. In 1873, the state legislature passed separate acts calling for the annexation of Charlestown, West Roxbury, Brighton, and Brookline; the first three were approved by voters of those towns, but Brookline firmly rejected annexation, 706-299, according to Puleo's *A City So Grand*.

STATION FOR WASHINGTON VILLAGE.

Residents of That Section Anxious That New York, New Haven & Hartford RR Establish One There.

Residents in the vicinity of Andrew sq, in that part of South Boston known as Washington village, are anxious that the New York, New Haven and Hartford railroad shall establish a station there for their convenience and thus provide opportunities for reaching that section of the city by railroad. For many years this has been a desire of people in that vicinity, but with the recent changes in the line of the railroad consequent upon the abolition of Dorchester av crossing and the raising of Swett, Boston sts and Dorchester av, thus bringing the tracks much nearer the square, the people are in hopes that the station will now be established.

With the end in view of securing this station at the earliest possible time, a petition was started today, to be presented to the proper authorities, asking for the location of a station. The petition will be in the store of Dr C. P. Flynn, corner of Preble st and Andrew sq, and, it is assured, will receive many signatures.

For many years the leading citizens of this section have been interested in this matter. When the old Washington village improvement association was in existence efforts were made, but without success.

By the street car lines it takes a very long time to reach that portion of the city, and with the poor accommodations that South Boston is subjected to generally the residents in the vicinity of Andrew sq are particular sufferers. Opportunities to reach their homes from the city by means of the railroad would be fully appreciated by the people there, and the building of the station would be a paying investment for the railroad.

With the tracks crossing Swett st, Boston st and Dorchester av, all close to Andrew sq, there will be an excellent chance to erect a small station suitable for the convenience of the people there. There is much vacant land on each of these streets, and it would require but a little expenditure to erect a building such as is necessary.

The residents of Washington Village intend to make every possible effort this time, and all possible influence will be used to get the station.

Boston Globe, **December 16, 1899.**

Schworm—Lowe.

Grace church, Washington village, South Boston, was well filled last evening, when Miss Bertha Lowe and Mr George M. Schworm, both very popular members of the parish, were married. The services were conducted by the rector, Rev W. S. W. Raymond, and the vested choir sang "The Voice that Brea hed O'er Eden" and "Rejoice, Ye Pure in Heart." The bride was gowned in white swiss muslin, and wore a veil. The bridesmaids were Miss Eva Schworm, sister of the groom, and Miss Edith Lowe, sister of the bride. They wore white muslin. Mr William Schworm, brother of the groom, was best man, and Mr Samuel Lowe, her uncle, gave the bride away. The ushers were Messrs Fred Hutton, William Douglas, Arthur Schworm and George Douglas. After the services in the church a reception was held at the residence of Mr Schworm, 32 Howells st. Mr and Mrs Schworm were the recipients of many handsome presents. They will reside at 54 Lonsdale st, Ashmont.

Boston Globe, **December 3, 1900.**

DEATH OF EDWARD MORGAN.

Well-Known Resident of Washington Village Passes Away at 89.

Edward Morgan, one of the oldest residents of Washington village, died at his home, 3 Gifford pl, yesterday morning.

Mr Morgan was born in Ireland 89 years ago and came to America in 1852. He became a resident of the Fort Hill district and a member of St Stephen's Episcopal church on Purchase st. When the great fire of 1872 destroyed St Stephen's, Mr Morgan removed with his family to Washington Village and was one of the first members of Grace church, which was started in 1871.

Since his arrival in Boston Mr Morgan had been connected with the iron business, of which James May was proprietor. He retired from active life about 12 years ago. He was a man of reserved disposition, and many an old resident of the village can testify to his generous qualities.

He leaves a wife and six children, one of whom, Miss Annie Morgan, has been a teacher in Grace church Sunday school ever since its formation.

Boston Globe, **November 29, 1900.**

After that, the annexation movement slowed, though Hyde Park was added in 1912. While Brookline never did become part of Boston even though it is surrounded by the city on three sides, it ceded two small pieces of land along the Charles River to Boston in the 1870s to help complete the filling of the Back Bay to Kenmore Square and to connect Brighton to Boston proper.

Like the rest of the city, Dorchester, South Boston, and Washington Village were transformed by the forces that led to annexation. In Dorchester, property values soared tenfold following annexation. The Irish, largely confined to the waterfront neighborhoods of Boston proper before the Civil War, moved across the channel in large numbers to South Boston; by the turn of the century, according to Thomas O'Connor's *South Boston, My Hometown*, more than eighty thousand people packed into South Boston, overwhelmingly first- or second-generation Irish,

DEATH OF JOHN D. FENTON.

Long Illness of Prominent South Boston Man Proves Fatal.

Ex-Representative John D. Fenton of South Boston died at his home, 35 Woodward st. Washington Village section, early this morning. He had been ill for a long time, but up to several months ago it was thought he might recover his former good health.

Mr Fenton was born in South Boston, where he attended the grammar schools, after which he entered the employ of the Boston Herald in the mailing department, where he was employed up to the time of his death.

Mr Fenton entered the political arena from ward 15, and served three years in the common council. Two years ago, with Hon William S. McNary, he was elected to the house of representatives from his ward. He always proved himself a faithful servant of the people of

THE LATE JOHN D. FENTON.

his ward, with whom he was extremely popular and well liked.

In the council of 1898 he served on the committees of collecting, street laying out and water department, mayor's address, Memorial day and municipal ownership.

Mr Fenton was a past president of the Boston newspaper mailers' union 1 and was a delegate from the union to the I. T. U. convention at Detroit in 1900.

For years he was a delegate to the Central labor union, attending many meetings and working hard for the success of organized labor. He was also a prominent member of the A. O. H., the Heptasophs and other organiza-

and almost exclusively Democratic. Washington Village, which was Boston's Ward 15 for political purposes, running from East and West Ninth Streets to the industrial areas along Dorchester Avenue and South Bay, "by this time was the largest single Irish enclave in Boston."

At the Dorchester border of Washington Village, a large Polish community made homes in the triple-deckers nearest the train depots. In 1891, forty years after it was named Washington Village, the area officially was renamed Andrew Square, in honor of John A. Andrew, governor of Massachusetts during the Civil War and a staunch Republican supporter of Abraham Lincoln. Andrew, at the age of forty-nine, died suddenly of apoplexy in 1867 after drinking tea in his Boston home.

As a new century approached, residents of the area had begun to grow concerned that the term "village" diminished it in the eyes

Boston Globe, **April 1, 1902.**

ton st.   Smitf s28

10 CHEAP HORSES.

1 PAIR SORRELS, weigh 2200, $75; 1 black
horse, weighs 1050, $40; 1 bay horse, weighs
1050, $30, and 6 other horses, weighing from
1000 to 1300; these horses are from 7 to 10
years old, are usefully sound and good workers;
been used by the Washington Village Mineral
Water Co this past season; are sold for no
fault, only as we have no further use for them;
also their harnesses and wagons; this property
will be sold cheap for cash, subject to a guarantee. Call at stable, 565 Dorchester av; tel
57-8 So Boston.   *

$85.00 BUY'S FRANK WILKES.

Boston Globe, September 28, 1902.

Atlantic av, opposite south union station. SuM*

WAGON WORTH LOOKING AT,

5 horses, used by the Washington Village
towel supply co, weigh from 1000 to 1200, war-
ranted sound and kind, good workers single or
double, will be sold cheap as we have closed
out the business; also the harnesses and wagons. Seen at residence 565 Dorchester av, Dor.*

Boston Globe, Nov, 25, 1900.

of fellow Bostonians and gave it less clout than it deserved. The *Boston Post* had noted in May 1891 that the area, despite having a population at the time of 16,459, was one of three wards in the city "without the benefit of parks." When the *Boston Daily Globe* reported that the Washington Village Improvement Association voted

20-22 Ellery Street, 1915. *Boston City Archives.*

to change its name to the Andrew Square Citizens' Association, it noted that "this district is no longer a village, but has filled out and spread so as to be an important part of composite Boston," and that the name "Washington Village" had "apparently outlived its usefulness."

In 1891, following a petition to the Boston Board of Alderman from the Washington Village Improvement Association, Alderman George von Lengerke Meyer proposed that "the square at the junction of Dorchester avenue and Dorchester, Swett [now Southampton], Boston and Preble streets be and the same is hereby named Andrew square." There was some confusion in the board of aldermen as to exactly which Andrew the square would be honoring; Alderman Thomas W. Flood first argued in February that the square would honor John F. Andrew, who at the time represented Washington Village in the US House of Representatives. Flood corrected himself a week later, after the motion was tabled, to inform the board that the honoree was John F. Andrew's father, John A. Andrew.

Despite some grumbling from a downtown alderman, Lewis G. Farmer, who feared that "if this thing keeps on, we will be appointing a committee to go through the city

Boston Globe, March 17, 1905.

and name every cross-road in Boston from Dedham to the North End," the board voted eight to four on March 2, 1891, to rename the area Andrew Square.

But the term "Washington Village" continued to be used informally well into the twentieth century, as place names that have worked their way into the culture often do; a *Boston Globe* story from 1924 describing new ward lines and boundaries in Boston referred to the new Ward 7 as including "South Boston South, and Washington Village."

The burgeoning populations of South Boston, Washington Village, Andrew Square, and all of Dorchester strained the transportation networks of the nineteenth century. Most of the neighborhoods were too close to the city center to benefit from the growth of the railroads at midcentury, but the

493-501 Southampton Street. 1911. *Boston City Archives.*

streetcar became a transportation lifeline. The first attempt to introduce public transportation was the horse-drawn "omnibus," which arrived in 1826, according to Sam Bass Warner Jr.'s *Streetcar Suburbs*. The omnibus, a sort of oversized urban stagecoach, typically carried nine passengers plus a driver, and cost too much to be of great value as a commuting vehicle for most working people. Nonetheless, the streets of Boston and South Boston were soon choking in omnibus traffic; according to the book *Boston in Motion* by Frank Cheney and Anthony M. Sammarco, the smelly, dirty, overcrowded vehicles were "the subject of almost daily newspaper editorials" in the early 1850s railing against their presence.

Fortunately, other technological solutions were on the horizon. The streets of South Boston began to be paved at midcentury; the first, in fact, was the

528–538 Dorchester Avenue, 1911. *Boston City Archives.*

Dorchester Turnpike (now Dorchester Avenue), which was paved all the way from West Fourth Street to today's Dorchester Avenue Bridge over the Fort Point Channel, in the vicinity of today's Broadway subway station. Paving led to the laying of steel rails, which brought horse-drawn streetcars to the neighborhood. One of the first, the Dorchester Avenue Railroad Company, was incorporated in 1854 to carry passengers from Dorchester's Lower Mills to the foot of State Street in downtown Boston along Dorchester Avenue. Eventually, according to O'Connor, five hundred miles of streetcar lines were laid within four miles of city hall, creating a crush of traffic as the lines converged downtown.

In 1872, an outbreak of horse influenza crippled the streetcar network and its livestock. Thousands of horses were killed or sickened; the street railway companies were reduced to hiring teams of men to pull the cars along

563–575 Dorchester Avenue, 1911. *Boston City Archives.*

the tracks to keep passengers moving. The cost of feeding and stabling such vast numbers of horses, and dealing with the estimated ten pounds of manure each horse generated per day, spurred the streetcar lines to consolidate operations, reduce competition, lower prices, and invest in electrification. By 1893, Brookline's Henry Whitney had merged most of the city's lines into his West End Street Railway Company, reduced his reliance on horses from eight thousand in 1887 to less than half that in 1893, electrified two-thirds of his 260 miles of track, and standardized prices on his lines to five cents a ride, according to Doug Most's *The Race Underground: Boston, New York, and the Incredible Rivalry that Built America's First Subway*. What he hadn't done—yet—was to reduce traffic by any significant degree. Doing that required him to persuade Boston to embark on a solution first

Fire Station, Andrew Square, 507-509 Southampton Street, 1911. *Boston City Archives.*

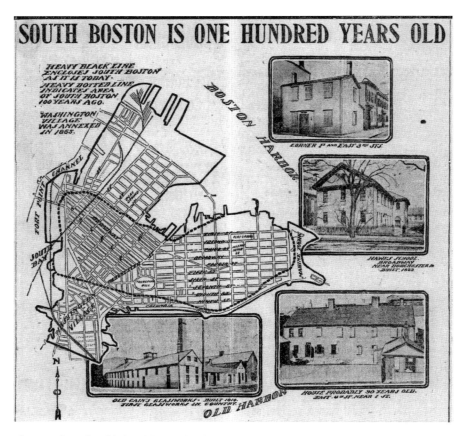

Boston Sunday Globe, **March 6, 1904.**

implemented in London in 1863, but yet to be attempted in America: the subway.

After this explosion of land making, land taking, and path making, Boston was now a very different place. Once a small peninsula of 750 acres, connected to the mainland by a narrow neck, the city now contained twenty-four thousand acres—thirty times its original size. From twenty-four thousand residents of primarily British lineage in 1800, the city a century later contained 560,000, composed largely of immigrants or the descendants of

599 Dorchester Avenue at Dexter Street, 1911. *Boston City Archives.*

---

immigrants from across Europe. A city where most business and personal relationships took place within a radius of what a human could comfortably walk or, occasionally, ride on horseback had become a commuting metropolis where many residents lived miles away, connected to work and social life by streetcars or railroads. The twentieth century, and the dominant role played by the automobile, would stretch the city even further and continue to reshape the historic corridor linking Dorchester and Boston.

Chapter 7. Decline and Resurgence

Like the streetcar lines, the railroads of New England also consolidated operations late in the century. In 1893, the independent Old Colony Railroad became a division of the New Haven Railroad. From as many as eighteen systems feeding Boston in the 1880s, three principal carriers emerged by 1900: the New Haven to the south, the New York Central to the west, and the Boston & Maine to the north. They also consolidated terminals. The New Haven abandoned Park Square in 1899 for South Station, as did the New York Central. The four lines that once converged from the north consolidated into North Union Station on Causeway Street in 1893, which was replaced by the North Station/Boston Garden complex in 1928 and, later, by today's North Station/TD Garden in 1995.

Once the streetcar lines consolidated and it became clear that Boston's first subway under Boston Common was a success, the need for public funding to raise the massive amounts of money required to tunnel beneath the city and extend subway lines outward led to the creation of the Boston Transit Authority, precursor of today's MBTA, in 1897. The transit authority and its successors eventually took over all responsibilities for subway and commuter rail service in eastern Massachusetts, but its first major project was to expand the subway system aggressively.

Electric streetcars on South Boston's streets connected Andrew Station and Broadway Station along Dorchester Avenue to

Lining up track near D Street on Old Colony Avenue, 1915.
Boston City Archives.

South Station in Boston, and from there all the way to Harvard Square in Cambridge. Marine Park, City Point, and Castle Island were likewise connected by streetcar to South Station. "The maze of streetcar lines made South Boston not just a convenient place to live but also a popular destination on summer weekends," according to author Anthony Sammarco's book *South Boston, Volume II.*

Dorchester Avenue was completely excavated in 1917 to build the Dorchester Tunnel, putting all the streetcar traffic from Andrew Square to Broadway Station underground. It eventually was linked underground to Ashmont Station in Dorchester and Harvard Square in Cambridge, transforming the formerly traffic-choked journey above ground into a speedy subterranean trip of fifteen minutes or less. But the construction was highly disruptive to the neighborhood; in 1916, the Boston Transit Commission ordered fifty-four families and ten businesses to vacate their holdings to build Andrew Square Station, and a number of other houses also were moved, according to author Frank Cheney's book *Boston's Red Line: Bridging the Charles from Alewife to Braintree.*

As early as 1926, the Metropolitan Planning Commission recommended that the expansion continue further outward, extending the Dorchester line out through Quincy to Braintree in the south, and north to Waltham. It would be almost half a

Doc. Tun. Drinking Fountain at junc. of Old Colony & Dorch. Aves.   Mar. 22, 1915.   681-D.

Drinking fountain at the Dorchester Tunnel at the junction of Old Colony and Dorchester avenues, 1915. *Boston City Archives.*

century before some of those ideas were acted on.

The subway project in South Boston set a pattern that was to be repeated time and again in the twentieth century around Boston: transportation projects took precedence over neighborhood residents. As the car became the dominant form

Construction of the Dorchester Tunnel north of 415 Dorchester Avenue, 1915. *Digital Commonwealth.*

of transportation in the middle of the twentieth century, investments in the rail lines that had been Boston's economic lifeblood for a hundred years slowed. The region's roadway network was ill-equipped to handle the flood of traffic created as car ownership became prevalent. Even in the 1920s, when barely one in five residents of Greater Boston owned a car, the public clamored for more roads. In 1925, a committee of the state legislature submitted a comprehensive report on the "intolerable conditions" that resulted from the "street problem in down-town Boston," according to the book *Boston's Central Artery*, by transportation expert Yanni Tsipis. That and a more detailed study in 1930 recommended construction of a major north-south artery to "open up parts of the down-town district" and "give general traffic relief."

Depression and war intervened, delaying any major public works projects as traffic conditions worsened. Smaller parkways—scenic roads that were meant to carry pleasure vehicles out for rides through natural areas and beaches—were built around the region, notably the Old Colony Parkway (today's Morrissey Boulevard) in Dorchester, in the 1920s. By the mid-1950s, the Old Colony Parkway was woefully undersized for the volume of traffic it carried into and out of Boston from the south every day. A 1952 *Boston Globe* article, "Expressway Priority Pledge Elates South Shore Drivers," described the Old Colony Parkway as the second most congested highway in the region.

Determined to break through the inertia and improve the region's roadways, Governor Robert F. Bradford in 1947 unveiled a comprehensive master plan for seven highways to radiate outward from an "inner belt" that would encircle the city, including a Southeast Expressway that would connect from Boston south to Quincy. Each of the highways would be two-hundred- to three-hundred-feet wide, and be routed, the *Globe* wrote, through "thinly populated districts." The total plan was projected to cost $677 million, or $7.8 billion in 2019 dollars. "I know this is nothing but a

Dorch. Tun. Sec. H. Dorchester Ave. Trench N. of Woodward St.   June 18, 1915

Trench for the Dorchester Tunnel north of Woodward Street on Dorchester Avenue, 1915. *Digital Commonwealth.*

dream," Bradford said, "but I want the people to know what we really need to do and what it is going to cost."

A year later, following the outlines of the state master plan, the legislature authorized a bond issue to begin the work. Traffic conditions in South Boston and the South Shore made the Southeast Expressway a high priority, and planners focused in on choosing a route. Strapped for cash, the New Haven Railroad offered up land along the Old Colony Railroad right-of-way it controlled along South Bay and through Washington Village, parallel to Dorchester Avenue. Though the original idea had been to follow the renamed Old Colony Boulevard (today's Morrissey Boulevard), planners quickly pounced on the railroad's offer. The site "seems to be a natural," the state's project engineer told the *Globe*.

Ellery Street, looking north from Southampton Street, 1915. *Boston City Archives.*

539 Dorchester Avenue, 1916. *Boston City Archives.*

As plans got more detailed, the need for the government to forcibly take and remove homes and businesses through the South Boston/Andrew Square corridor became more obvious. The original plan called for the taking of 524 homes; a revised plan issued in 1954 cut that number to 150. The final plan, settled on in 1954, displaced 150 families and another thirty-five commercial or industrial firms, including Skinner Organ Co., which built some of the world's great pipe organs and employed 250 people in a factory near today's JFK/UMass Red Line MBTA station.

The new Southeast Expressway and its connecting highway through downtown Boston, the Central Artery, were hailed as a "dream road" when they opened to traffic in 1959. A *Globe* reporter clocked his drive from the newspaper's newly opened headquarters on Morrissey Boulevard to the Lynnfield/Peabody town line north of Boston at thirty-two minutes at the height of rush hour—a saving of fourteen minutes. "The trip was a breeze," reporter Ronald Wysocki wrote. "It was smooth and continuous. ... With the

Expressway, there were no nerve-wracking traffic jams, no twisting and turning, no mapping of battle strategy to find the quickest way home. It was just straight ahead, all the way."

A week after the highway opened, the New Haven Railroad, unsuccessful at keeping its state subsidy and now facing major competition, ended its passenger service to the South Shore and Plymouth, which had originated with the Old Colony Railroad in 1845. The MBTA eventually restored Red Line service to Quincy in 1971 and to Braintree in 1980. It revived commuter service along the Old Colony lines to Plymouth in 1997 and to Greenbush in 2007.

Even as the state poured money into major public works projects, it was not enough to stem Boston's serious economic decline. In the first few

Excavating the Dorchester Tunnel between Dexter Place and Dorchester Avenue, 1916. *Digital Commonwealth.*

Dor. Tun. Sec. J. Excavation bet. Dexter Pl. and Dorch. Ave, looking N. June 28, 1916. #1170-D.

Excavating the Dorchester Tunnel between Dexter Place and Dorchester Avenue, 1916. *Digital Commonwealth.*

---

decades of the twentieth century, the Boston economy "hollowed out," according to *The Atlas of Boston History*, edited by Nancy S. Seasholes. What was the nation's second-busiest port in 1900 had fallen to sixth by 1920. The basic problem Boston had faced since colonial times asserted itself once again: While Boston had railroads, port facilities, and infrastructure to move goods around, it had no underlying economic base. Its farms and fields produced little of value, and its transportation was isolated from the fertile grain- and food-producing regions to the west. Its iron foundries and shoe and textile companies were located far from their sources of raw goods, so the factories relocated to find cheaper labor and better access to their supplies. The piano business was devastated by the invention of the radio; Prohibition shuttered breweries and distilleries around the city, as it did all across the country.

As the jobs moved out, so did the people. The city's population dropped 13 percent in the 1950s, a higher percentage than any other major city in the United States. It fell another 30 percent between 1950 and 1980, back roughly to the level where it was at the turn of the century. Like the rest of the city, the South Boston neighborhood was emptying out as well, losing 20 percent to 25 percent of its population. "Boston by 1950 was in the middle of economic contraction and on the brink of population collapse," wrote former Boston Redevelopment Authority chief economist John Avault in *The Atlas of Boston History*.

Dor. Tun. Sec. J. Excavating in Andrew Sq. looking N'W'ly. May 20, 1916. #1116-D

Excavating for the Dorchester Tunnel in Andrew Square, 1916. *Boston City Archives.*

Dor. Tun. Sec. J, Moving "3-flatter" along Dexter St. looking N.W'ly.   *June 7, 1916. #1153-D.*

Moving a "three-flatter" (triple decker) along Dexter Street to make room for the Dorchester Tunnel. *Boston City Archives.*

Moving and altering buildings on Dexter Place for the Dorchester Tunnel, 1916. *Boston City Archives.*

For a time at the turn of the century, the state and the city continued its traditional method to stoke growth: create more land. On the South Boston waterfront, the ambitious Commonwealth Flats project to fill in hundreds of acres of land along the harbor and build new port facilities was begun in 1916, but the land stood empty and vacant for the rest of the century. In the 1930s, Castle Island was connected to the mainland, and more port facilities developed in that area of the harbor.

On the channel side of South Boston, at the edges of the old Washington Village, South Bay became one of the major new swaths of land to be created. Despite having been dredged in the nineteenth century to provide fill for the South End, the wharves of South Bay never became a significant economic engine. Like the Back Bay, the stagnant waters of South Bay became a filthy, polluted eyesore. Beginning in 1926, the state issued a series of reports recommending completely filling in South Bay and Fort Point Channel south of Dorchester Avenue for sanitary reasons. The water in the bay, the state wrote, was "badly discolored," with "occasional masses of floating sludge usually present," according to *Gaining Ground*. "Gas bubbles [rise] abun-

ANNUAL DANCE IN SOUTH BOSTON

Washington Village Club Event Tomorrow

The Washington Village Club, one of the popular organizations of the Peninsular District, will have its annual dancing party tomorrow evening at the Perkins Post Hall, East Broad-

UPPER—LOUISE ALLEN
LOWER—MARGARET O'LEARY.

way, South Boston. Plans for this event have been under way for several weeks and indications point to a successful event. Prior to the dancing there will be a program of varied talent. A collegiate dancing contest will feature, with prizes to be awarded to the winning couple.

Walter F. Murray is chairman of the committee, assisted by Frank Connell, John Lyons and Christopher Lee. The other club members will be aids.

A group of young women assisting in the plans includes the Misses Margaret O'Leary, Anne Sullivan, Mary Kehoe, Doris Murray and Louise Allen.

Boston Globe, April 18, 1929.

dantly from the bottom ... [and] the odor in the immediate neighborhood of the channel [is] offensive." The project stalled, but eventually the bay was filled to create land for the burst of road-building activity in the 1950s. The rest of the land would remain vacant until 1993, when much of it was developed into the South Bay shopping center.

Crisscrossed by highway projects, excavated for subway tunnels, and abandoned by railroads, Washington Village/Andrew Square lost much of its residential character, despite close proximity to the Andrew Square and Broadway subway stops. And though the major foundries and factories of the nineteenth century died off or moved, the neighborhood's proximity to Boston and its industrial character continued to serve as a home for the plain, unglamorous businesses that provide jobs and services that keep

Dorchester Tunnel. Birdseye view of Andrew Square Surface Station, 1917. *Boston Globe Library Collection at the Northeastern University Archives and Special Collections.*

SAW A HORSELESS CARRIAGE IN 1870

To the Editor of the Post:

Sir—Quite recently I saw in the columns of the Post a cut and description of what was described as the first horseless carriage, and it was dated as being in use about 1880 or 1882.

Somewhere about 1870, and not later than 1872, I saw in South Boston a vehicle of similar construction. I was living in "Washington Village" at that time, and the carriage was seen on Dorchester avenue, beyond Dorchester street.

The maker had taken a common open buggy, and, removing the shafts, had attached an upright bar and on top had placed a wheel or a lever by which to do the steering. The rear wheels had been made fast to the axle, and in the axle there were two small cranks to which small horizontal engines were attached. The boiler—for of course it was a steam carriage—was a small upright one, with the firing door at the rear. It was necessary to stop from time to time to fire up and oil the bearings. The throttle was the usual kind on small stationary engines—just a common globe valve with a small wheel, and to stop or start the engines the driver had to reach back of the seat. It was a crude affair, but it could make good time, and could scare the horses met on the road as well as a modern noisy chain-driven gasolene truck can scare a horse from "way back" today.

I thought this might interest some one, so am taking the liberty of sending it in. I only wish I were artist enough to make a drawing of it as I remember it. I was then a boy in my early teens and quite a mechanic in a way, so took in details that might have escaped me otherwise.   X. P. Y.

Bryant Pond, Me.

Boston Post, October 24, 1920.

cities running. The Karas family moved its Karas & Karas Glass Company to Dorchester Avenue in the 1930s and has outlasted several of its competitors in the area. Employing about two hundred people, it provides glass for the high-end residential and commercial towers in Boston and Cambridge—buildings such as the New Balance complex in Allston, Novartis and Genzyme in Kendall Square, Harvard Business School's Tata Hall, and the Omni Boston Hotel at the Seaport.

Daniel Marr & Son Company was established at 384 Dorchester Avenue in 1898 and has been based in Washington Village while spreading throughout South Boston as it has grown. The company now includes six divisions. The original Daniel Marr & Son erects steel and concrete at major buildings throughout the region. Early in the twentieth century, it helped build Commonwealth Pier (today's Seaport World Trade Center) and Braves Field, which partly survives today

New York New Haven & Hartford Railroad Station, South Boston, 1913, *Boston City Archives.*

as Boston University's Nickerson Field. It has added to the Boston skyline on projects such as Rowes Wharf, Millennium Place, and Boston University's Student Village. Marr Crane & Rigging provides cranes, construction elevators, and riggings to construction sites; Marr Scaffolding Company similarly provides scaffolding at construction sites and temporary or permanent grandstands for major events. Isaac Blair & Co., established in 1820 and purchased in 1969, provides equipment and services to shore up and brace historic structures during renovations and to lift buildings off their foundations when repairs are needed.

For more than eighty years, until it was demolished in 2017 to make way for the Washington Village development, the 120-foot tall smoke stack of Crown Uniform and Linen Service, formerly known as Loyal Crown Linen Service, dominated the landscape around Dorchester Avenue, with the

Andrew Square, circa 1915. *Boston Globe Library Collection at the Northeastern University Archives and Special Collections.*

words "Loyal Crown" embedded in white brick down the length of the stack. Crown has been in the hands of the Spilios family since 1914, when brothers Athans and Demosthenes Spiliotopoulos came from Greece and started a business delivering coats and aprons by horse and wagon, and even by bicycle, to the food establishments and fish piers of Boston. The family acquired a linen service from Worcester in the 1930s and built their own laundry, including the smoke stack, in the neighborhood in 1933. The company grew and expanded throughout the twentieth century to provide linens and uniforms to hospitals, biotechnology facilities, research facilities, and restaurants, and today employs about 225 people. The company, still owned by the third- and fourth-generations of the Spilios family, moved to Brockton in 2017 to expand and make way for the redevelopment of Washington Village.

Andrew Square Station, 1920s. *Boston City Archives.*

Dorchester Heights from South Boston, 1926. *Boston Globe Library Collection at the Northeastern University Archives and Special Collections.*

Winthrop Printing Co. was established in 1916 to provide printing and publishing services to the mutual fund industry, banks, insurance companies, and retailers. As the financial services industry grew in Boston, it churned out millions of pages of annual and quarterly reports, prospectuses, and other documents, and the major players turned to Winthrop for its needs. With customers such as Fidelity Investments, Putnam Investments, Pioneer Funds, John Hancock Funds, and State Street Corp., the firm's sales grew to $25 million annually by the 1990s. As the need for printed reports in the financial services industry dwindled, business dried up, and the firm filed for bankruptcy after the turn of the century.

A small residential community survived at the base of the triangle between Dorchester Avenue and Old Colony Avenue, crowded in by commercial and industrial businesses and centered on the cross streets of Woodward and Middle Streets. Just across Old Colony from that enclave sat Kelly's Cork 'N Bull Tavern, the neighborhood's link to South Boston's less savory, more sinister past. A "bucket of blood," as former South Boston State Representative Brian P. Wallace described it, the Cork 'N Bull was owned for more than forty years by Martin "Mutt" Kelly. Kelly, who also owned downtown Boston's venerable Durgin-Park restaurant and a jazz club in the South End, reportedly began his career as a smuggler of booze during Prohibition. After World War II he turned to the bar and restaurant business, acquiring the bar that would become Kelly's Cork 'N Bull in 1968 and Durgin-Park in 1977.

Michael Patrick MacDonald, a former South Boston resident and author of *All Souls: A Family Story from Southie,* wrote in the *Globe* in 2007 about the dark side of the fierce loyalty that residents of neighborhoods such as Charlestown and South Boston developed about their hometowns. "When I lived there, the summer streets teemed with children playing in hydrants," he wrote. "Neighbors all knew each other, and loyalty reigned supreme.

Plowing snow on Dorchester Avenue for St. Patrick's Day Parade, March 12, 1969. *Boston Globe Library Collection at the Northeastern University Archives and Special Collections.*

Businesses on Old Colony Avenue, Nov. 19, 1978. *Boston Globe Library Collection at the Northeastern University Archives and Special Collections.*

Then again, that same loyalty reinforced a code of silence that might mean getting killed at Kelly's Cork 'N Bull Tavern in front of hundreds of silent witnesses."

The most notorious murder to occur at the Cork 'N Bull took place in 1997, when brothers Joseph and Daniel Downey stabbed James W. Murphy in a rear hallway of the bar at 1:30 on a Saturday morning in March, supposedly in retaliation for an argument between Murphy and Joseph Downey a week before at the South Boston Saint Patrick's Day parade.

Violence was not uncommon at the Cork 'N Bull; a man had been shot twice in the leg while sitting in a booth there in 1995, and a fight in the bar a year later allegedly led to the fatal shooting of another South Boston man. But the Murphy stabbing was tied up in court for more than a decade, as the facts of the case became entangled with issues of an unfair trial for the brothers because their lawyers participated in a PBS Frontline documen-

tary about criminal justice. A state court ruled that the brothers were hesi-
tant to talk freely to their lawyers because the lawyers wore microphones
at trial. Daniel Downey later pleaded guilty to manslaughter, and Joseph
Downey's murder conviction was overturned, following a ruling that the
judge improperly excluded the public from the jury selection portion of his
second trial.

Near the end of the twentieth century, the economic forces that had pun-
ished Boston for almost a hundred years began to turn in the city's favor.
Despite the region's continuing lack of raw natural and manufacturing resources, the one asset the city has never lacked—brainpower—reasserted
itself. The renaissance first began in the outer regions of Greater Boston,
where a high-technology belt of computer hardware companies, led by
Digital Equipment Corp. and Data General, piggybacked off the technological research coming out of institutions such as the Massachusetts Insti-
tute of Technology and the innovations such as the instant camera pouring
out of Edwin Land's Polaroid Corp. Government-funded defense research
also played a major role in spinning off new companies, followed in later
decades by government-funded medical research in the labs and clinics
operated by the powerhouse hospitals associated with Harvard's Medical
School—Brigham & Women's Hospital, Beth Israel Hospital, and Massachusetts General Hospital.

As the century turned, the economy was based even less on the items
Massachusetts made, such as mainframe computers, and more on the
ideas and intellectual property generated in Boston's labs and classrooms.
The need for acres of space in suburban industrial parks lessened. In Boston's new brain-based economy, residents and workers preferred the cul-
tural and intellectual stimulation that cities provide and the serendipity of
bumping into like-minded researchers, software writers, and bloggers in
local coffee shops and restaurants. As more alternative transportation so-

lutions developed, younger graduates were far less likely than their parents to own a car, relying instead on the explosive growth of car-sharing services such as Uber and Lyft.

Businesses and residents flocked back to the city in increasing numbers. From a low of 562,944 residents in 1980, Boston's population rose 25 percent over the next forty years, to an estimated 694,583 in 2018. The economic and real estate revival first took root in the historic core of Boston, where property values rose and building activity mushroomed. In the first two decades of the twenty-first century, as Boston grew, the Dorchester Avenue corridor in South Boston, which had evolved into a collection of smaller one- and two-story commercial and industrial enterprises such as paint shops and glass-repair facilities sprinkled among the few surviving larger businesses, began to look more appealing for residential purposes. The same amenities that had drawn businesses and residents to the area since colonial times—proximity to downtown Boston, multiple transportation options such as the Broadway and Andrew Square MBTA stations, and the attraction of nearby beaches and harbors—led residents, city officials, and developers to reimagine what the neighborhood could be.

The City of Boston and Mayor Martin J. Walsh identified a 144-acre swath of land encompassing the historic outlines of the old Washington Village neighborhood as ripe for redevelopment in 2015 and kicked off the efforts to transform the area. The plan, released a year later, acknowledged that the industrial jobs that the neighborhood has provided for two centuries had shrunk dramatically in the last few decades of the twentieth century and called for more housing, offices, laboratories, and green space.

Ireland's St. Joseph's Band performs in the St. Patrick's Day Parade, with Dorchester Heights in the background, March 22, 1989. *Boston Globe Library Collection at the Northeastern University Archives and Special Collections.*

The demolition of the iconic smoke stack for Crown Uniform and Linen Service, a landmark on Dorchester Avenue for almost a century, December 1, 2017. *Photo by Tom Palmer.*

Developers responded instantly. In the next few years, two major firms that had acquired almost forty acres along Dorchester Avenue and Old Colony Avenue, Core Investments and National Development, introduced plans to spend several billion dollar in the corridor.

In 2015, developer Dave Pogorelc and his company, Core Investments, filed plans with the City of Boston to replace five acres of low-slung commercial and industrial buildings with nine buildings containing 656 units of housing, both apartments and condominiums, as well as retail, surrounding a village green. It was the first public park ever proposed for the neighborhood; as the Boston Post noted in 1891 and as remains true today, there are no parks in the neighborhood. Pogorelc reached back into the area's rich history and christened the $400 million development "Washington Village," the name that had been attached to the neighborhood from the time it became a residential enclave in the 1850s until it went out of use in the early part of the twentieth century. In 2018, Core Investments announced that it had partnered with one of Boston's largest commercial developers, Samuels & Associates, to move the project forward. Samuels, founded by developer Steve Samuels, got its start redeveloping the South

Bay shopping center before turning its attention to Boston's Fenway neighborhood, where it has built or renovated several major residential and office buildings along Boylston Street. In 2019, Samuels and Core received approval to expand the number of residential units to 746, while slightly reducing the retail space and surface parking. The revision moved the public greenspace out to the front along Damrell and Alger Streets to make the village green more visible.

Core also bought up more than twenty acres of land on the western side of Dorchester Avenue, between the street and the Amtrak and MBTA rail lines, for a second, even more ambitious buildout of six million to eight million square feet of new construction, which it calls "On the Dot." The project is expected to be about one-third residential and two-thirds office and laboratory space, to complement the housing and retail it plans to build with Samuels across the way. And further north along Dorchester Avenue, closer to the Broadway MBTA station, National Development has acquired about twelve acres and filed plans for the first phase of its project, known as 333 Dorchester Avenue. National Development proposes to build housing, office space, and retail space, along with some open space on its property.

By 2030, this billion-dollar investment in the neighborhood should help fulfill the vision for the area first outlined by the Andrew Square Civic Association in 2005: "To bring economic vitality to the Andrew Square triangle, by creating a walkable neighborhood with community-serving businesses, upgrading a housing stock, striking a healthy balance between residents and industrial users, providing healthier food options, encouraging lower impact and less polluting industrial uses, and improving the quality of life for residents."

Chapter 8. Voices of the Neighborhood

Joey Karas, Chief Executive
Karas & Karas Glass Company

Our family business, Karas & Karas Glass Company, has been in business since approximately 1924. It was started by my grandfather and his first cousin. When we started, I think we were on Sherman Avenue back in the '20s. We were out in Squantum and Quincy in the '30s. We moved into South Boston and built a state-of-the-art building on Dorchester Avenue in about 1930-something. That's at 455 Dorchester Avenue. We expanded. We are a wholesale glass fabricator and distributor, as well as what they used to call a contract glazier. Today we use the words "building enveloper" because we wrap buildings in glass and other material primarily in the Boston area. We're a union company and a proud union company. We expanded along Dorchester Ave. because it was a good place to do business, so we're now at 455 Dorchester Ave., 297 Dorchester Ave., 10 Alger Street, and a couple of other addresses that are not recorded on deeds, but they're there.

This neighborhood has been great for us. We operate here. It's easy access to downtown Boston where we do most of our work. It's central to New England where we do most of our distribution. I've worked here since I was sixteen. I'm sixty-one. I don't live here. I would come in from the suburbs, show up at eight in the morning, leave at five-thirty in the afternoon. So my life wasn't as a South Boston resident. It was as a South Boston employee. But my whole family has been here—cousins, uncles, aunts, sisters, brothers, nephews. And we see a change coming.

When I came into South Boston, I was sort of a sheltered suburban kid. I would come in here, and I would see a neighborhood that was primarily made up of very hard-working people. I worked side by side with many of them. Most of the people that worked at Karas Glass were from the neighborhood or from the area, whether it be our shop workers, our field workers, office staff. It was a very good experience. They were very family-oriented.

Me personally, I started probably coming here around 1972. I came here before that as a young man on Saturday afternoons with my dad just to play with his adding machine or things like that. We are the largest glass business in New England—architectural glass, not auto glass. Dorchester Ave. was always an industrial, working street. It was never a retail street. It was never a residential street. It was never anything different than that. There were a lot of industrial companies side by side, whether it be the electrical supply or the crane people, a lot of automotive shops. There were three glass houses on Dorchester Ave. up until about 1980. There was Karas Glass, there was Economy Glass, and there was Guardian Glass Industries. Guardian was at 365 [Dorchester Avenue], and Economy Glass was over on Albany Street. Guardian is a global glass company, one of the five biggest in the world. They just had a distribution house at 365 Dorchester Ave. that they eventually moved out of.

Economy Glass was an offshoot of our company. We sold it to the Pearl family back in the '40s. It went out of business during the economic downturn, I'm going to say, probably late '80s. All the equipment left the area, and the Marr family bought the property.

I've been told for the past ten years, and I've certainly witnessed it, that South Boston, not necessarily Dorchester Ave., but East and West Broadway, all the numbered and lettered streets have gone from three families who had lived there, grandparents on one floor, parents on the next floor, those have all become high-end residential. Both my children lived in South Boston. They're now twenty-seven and thirty. My son still lives on West Second Street, and my daughter lived on Dorchester Ave. until about four years ago. I'll never forget when I said to my wife, "Our children are moving to South Boston to live." She was a little shocked.

They like living here. At five o'clock at night when I look at Broadway Station, that's when I can really tell what's happening. And I see a lot of young working people coming from downtown on the Red Line and getting off and going left, right. It's an amazing difference from what I saw as a young man when I ... at night I thought, "I better get out of here."

Real estate prices have soared. We haven't sold anything. I know what we paid when we came here in the '40s, and we bought quite a bit in the '70s. I've seen the price skyrocket because developers see a future. I agree with them. It doesn't seem to have stopped.

We'd like to continue to operate our business in Boston. We're just finding the real estate—the term is "higher and better use"—all over the place. I'm going to be the beneficiary, but I'm not looking to be the beneficiary, if that makes any sense. I'm just as happy the way things are. I don't have to move. The prices encourage us to take advantage of this opportunity. But we are an expanding business. We also operate down in Stoughton, Mass. So, most of our workforce now which once lived in South Boston all lives in the South Shore, down in Middleton and Pembroke and Rockland and those neighborhoods. So, our workforce is down there even though we do our work in Boston. We'd like to build a big modern facility down there. And I think we would do that whether the prices were going up or not.

We'll always have a presence in Boston. We will always have a presence in either Mattapan or Newmarket or South Boston. We're involved in a lot of construction work in Boston, which forces us to meet with the owners, architects, so we would always have a presence here.

We engineer, help design, buy, and install the material, whether it be glass, stone, composite aluminum. Most of our work is within a one-square-mile radius of here. We work in the Seaport now. We work at Brighton Landing now. We work in Kendall Square quite a bit.

Currently in the Seaport we finished two buildings, Vertex. We finished over in Kendall Square, Novartis and Genzyme over the years. We've built three buildings for Genzyme. Right now we're going to be building at the new Seaport Hotel, the Omni Seaport Hotel. We're going to be building the St. Regis at the old Whiskey Priest building. We built 50 Liberty, which is right on the waterfront. It's a condominium in that neighborhood. We did four out of five buildings at New Balance. We did their sideways skyscraper, or "sneaker" as we like to call it.

We built the Bruins practice facility. We're about to build [New Balance's] track and field facility. We do a lot of work for Harvard, MIT, Northeastern, and BU over the years. It's very rare we leave the Boston area. We do a lot of work at Logan Airport. We built those sky bridges that go from the parking garages. And that's as an installer. We're also the wholesale or distribution house to about six hundred glass users in all five New England states and the Albany, New York, market. Including administrative, shop, and field, we average about two hundred people working out of our office in Boston. That's about 150 union jobs in Boston.

In Stoughton I've got about fifty industrial people.

I used to be young. Now I'm old. I am the sole Karas who's in charge of the business. My dad is ninety, comes in every day. He's still our treasurer. And then I have a son, twenty-seven. My son Ben works for me. We have two or three families that represent about 30 percent of our workforce, all related, not related to me. There's an Argus family where we probably have ten or fifteen cousins, and there's a Wyatt family. A lot of times we want to call ourselves Argus & Wyatt Glass, not Karas & Karas because they do a lot more than we do. I am the CEO of the company, but I have two hundred associates that do a great job. I'm very fortunate. My dad was more of an engineer, architect, builder. My uncle, my father's brother Arthur, was more of a salesman. A lot of people know Arthur. Arthur was more socially out there. He had my role, which was more of a sales role.

You know, what's changed—on Dorchester Ave. we have a lot of suppliers or partners. Marr and Shaughnessy would supply us with cranes. Smith Machine would do our machine work. Other companies that are beginning to move.

It's hard for me to find employees who live close by because most of the kids who walk by work downtown in the financial services or accounting. They don't want to take this. ...It's a great job, but we don't find a lot of kids who can walk to work. I would say twenty-five years ago, all of our employees either lived or had lived in South Boston. They all had great handwriting because they'd learn Mrs. Palmer's cursive. We've lost all that. It was amazing. If I did something wrong, and they were twenty years older than me, they would still hit me with a ruler, and I was their boss.

Karas & Karas Glass plans just to stay and to grow and to continue to be active in the skinning or enveloping or installing of glass in buildings in Boston and act as a glass wholesaler, distributor, and fabricator to the glazing industry throughout New England. We've hired a lot of young kids to come on board and try to get the company younger. We've got a great mix of people with a lot of experience and a lot of people we've trained. What we do today is much more complicated than what we used to do, and it requires a different educational level of my employees than it used to. We used to do a lot of small storefront work. I could name jobs we did in the '30s and '40s and '50s which are much different than what we do today. We're the only union distributor left in New England. At one time there were probably half a dozen. We may be the only distributor left in Massachusetts.

My grandfather was the entrepreneur. My father and uncle were very good at building the business, but they built it slowly. And they paid for everything. They bought the land. They bought the trucks. They bought the equipment. They maintained the relationships. When I came on board, I was lucky enough to maybe be a little more aggressive and surround myself with some more aggressive people and try to grow it. The cost of entry into our business is not that easy. Nobody really wants to buy all that equipment, all that glass. The percentage return isn't all that great. Luckily, we do a big volume in business.

I don't remember [this neighborhood] being anything different than industrial. Everybody was building something, making something, fixing something. I said earlier, when I was maybe sixteen, I would drive my mom to work. My mom worked at Karas Glass, and I would enter Dorchester Ave. by the post office, drive down Dorchester Ave. to drop her off at work. I remember them closing it off at one point. And I think that's one of the things that slowed this neighborhood down. Dorchester Ave. was a main thoroughfare from downtown Boston all the way into Dorchester, Quincy. And to this day it's shut down, and I don't know why. I mean, it's right along the channel. It's a beautiful thoroughfare. If I were riding a bicycle, which I like to do, I'd like to ride up and down. I've recently moved back to the city. So, I technically live in South Boston, even though I live in the Seaport.

This was the industrial section and served the city of Boston. It was very close. We're less than a half mile from downtown Boston. We could get our goods and services there quickly. I'd like to operate here indefinitely.

We've been building big buildings for a long time. Some of the old buildings that I forget the names, because we go by addresses. But whether it be One Beacon we were involved with or a lot of business over at Harvard. We've been the glazier at Fenway Park forever. We've been the glazier at Gillette Stadium. We've been the glazier at Boston College at their sports facility. We've been doing jobs as big as Boston has been doing. We've grown with Boston. We were never a storefront guy. We never did the first floor. We always liked to do the towers.

To this day we're the maintenance contractor on the John Hancock Building and have been since the glass first broke. We didn't install it. We didn't reinstall it, but we maintain it to this day, probably two or three times a year.

Typically, glass is liquid turned to solid. It's got these little nickel sulfide stones in them. They expand and contract in the heat. So, in the summertime, most buildings lose a piece of what we call lighted glass. No one thinks about the ones that aren't John Hancock because they're not famous. But I remember being about twelve years old, and if my dad wasn't around, I would get the call at home. There was a little cheat sheet next to his bed. We had to get six men there by 6 a.m. or 6 p.m. that day. That was really my first glass job, I guess, other than cleaning up or scrubbing stuff. To this day it still goes on. Back then they had two men with binoculars, searching, going back and forth watching the glass in the Hancock looking for a defect. Today it's all computerized. If they find a defect, they actually reverse their [ventilation] system to suck everything in.

Our comfort zone is about a twenty- to thirty-story building. Having a Boston base has been good for us. Having a South Boston base has been good for us. We're thrilled to be residents of South Boston. I'm here ten hours a day, five days a week. My grandfather was a Boston resident. My father was a Boston resident. We have just become Boston residents. I think this is great for Boston, what's happening. I think in the long run, this is so close to downtown that if there's good housing, good shopping, good things to go along with it, what's needed, I think this is going to be an amazing residential, working neighborhood, very similar to Boylston Street in the Fenway, which I think had a similar renaissance. East Boston, I see it happening. Up in Somerville I see it happening. I should've bought a thousand buildings twenty years ago while I was watching out the window, but I didn't. I always looked in, not out.

Linda Zablocki, President
Andrew Square
Civic Association

My father is second genera-tion. Both my maternal and pater-nal grandparents came over from Poland. My mother was born in a coal-miners' town in Pennsylva-nia. My father was born here in Boston. He lived in a three-family house on Dexter Street. This house is still there and is currently owned by the tenants who have occupied the third floor most of my life.

One of my father's brothers, Bill, got married and moved into the first-floor apartment. As it was the custom in those days, family lived within close proximity of each other, often residing on the same street, even in the same house. I remember as a child we would always have family gatherings, and sometimes there were fifty of us in two small rooms. How the hell did we do it? I don't know because everybody needs their own space now; they need a separate bedroom and bathroom. When they were growing up, they had at one time three people in a bed. That's what you did then because that's all you had room for. But they didn't have it easy, and this is all what my fa-ther has told me over the years. I feel it was better then because you had to adjust to living with other people and their idiosyncrasies.

My dad passed away in 2000. There is a Chippewas Athletic Club down in Andrew Square that he was a charter member of, along with his brother Bill and a dozen other men who established this athletic club. My understand-ing is that it was one of the first semi-pro teams. They used to play in Fenway Park. They wore leather helmets! It's a club, a men's club. Right in back of where my mother's house is on Glover Court. As a matter of fact, when we bought the house you would have to walk around the block to get to the club. My father put up a fence and put a gate in the fence so we didn't have to walk around the block. He would just go through the gate and down a small ladder.

Growing up, I remember seeing the circus animals coming down Dorchester Avenue off the trains. They would march the elephants and the big animals to the Boston Garden, as far as I can recall. There was a piece of land known as the junkyard that was behind my father's house. During his younger days (he was born in 1922), they used to have the circuses there every year, right on Dorchester Avenue. The animals came through South Station by train. My dad would tell us that when the circus was over and everything was gone, they would go over there and go sift their hands through the sawdust to find the loose change that fell.

Then, you had the trains that went by there, and there were the coal cars. They used to call my Uncle Bill "Cokie." The story is he was tall enough to reach up to grab the coal off the train. The other ones had to wait for it to fall and they would follow the trains and get the coal to heat the house on Dexter Street. Well, the trains run behind the property, and Dexter Street runs off of Dorchester Avenue, so it was close.

My mother and father met while my mother was babysitting for my father's brother Bill's children. My mother was a cheerleader and he was a football player for the Chippewas, how convenient. My father went to St. Mary's— Our Lady of Czestochowa is the proper name of it. It's closed now, but the Polish church is still operating. My mother went to public school, and I do know that she went to Jeremiah E. Burke. She was very good in pole vaulting, but once she got to the high school, women were restricted from many things in those days. My father never graduated from Southie High. He got drafted and fought in World War II. He eventually got his diploma, but it was well after World War II when he returned home.

He didn't talk about the war much. He was a medic and we couldn't even talk at the table about a cut or a scab, he would get nauseous. I was like, "How the hell are you a medic?" But I know that he was in France during the war. He was commander of the Kosciuszko Post of the Veterans of Foreign Wars for years. They had a lot more VFW posts for the veterans around. A lot of them are closing up. It's sad. He did just his time in the army. He didn't make a career out of it or anything else. When he came back, he worked for Marr Companies down the end of our street. He walked home for lunch every day. Finally, he got accepted into the tin knockers union. That's what they're called, sheet metal workers. They did work all around. I remember him telling us that up on top of the Museum of Science there's a funny-looking design with a ball and a sphere with a point on it. That was done at his job. I don't know who he was working for at the time, but he always used to point that out: "I helped make that." It used to be so much more in the neighborhoods than just buildings. More community. There was so much more life. There were pizza parlors, and not like these. You would sit down and eat, and have things other than pizza. Mostly conversations, this is when people spoke to each other and looked each other in the eye—no texting then!

In the neighborhood, you had people watching for you all the time. Everybody knew what you were doing. There was no sneaking out or anything. You had to go way far away to do something that you knew you weren't supposed to be doing. You get in the house and your mother knew what you did before you even walked in the door because the neighbor would call and Mom would say, "You know, I spoke to ...," and they had the right to speak to you and reprimand you. Now, you can't open your mouth. It takes a village, I do believe that, and that has been lost.

I don't know exactly what year my parents connected, but they got married in '51. In '61, they bought the house on Glover Court, which brings me to Andrew Square where my father originally was from. I think I was about ten. Now there's more development activity in this neighborhood than most neighborhoods. We're probably equal with the waterfront, only in a smaller dimension. Anything that can be built on in South Boston is being bought, and there isn't a lot that's for sale up in the other spots. Now, you've got more around here. There's subway service, there's the beach, there's everything here. We are located even better than City Point. City Point you would need to take the bus to get to a subway.

If you look at Old Colony Avenue and you look at Dorchester Avenue and you look what's in between, it's the same thing you see right down over here. If you just look right next door, it's almost all industrial, low industrial or whatever. Not a lot of residential. On Dorchester Avenue, we have what we used to call the junkyard. Dexter Street residents have always abutted that industrial property, that's how close everything is. That junkyard had big piles of metal. You'd hear the big magnets picking up and dropping cars three, four stories high. You used to wipe your windowsills every day, because they were so full of rust. The rag would be dark brown from the residue on the windowsills.

I have one sister and three brothers. It's almost like two separate families because there's eleven years between me and my sister. But when we moved into Glover Court, we lived on the first floor. While there, my father would be doing over the second and third floors after work and on the weekends. We would eventually move up there to have the attic bedrooms. Downstairs we were in one tiny bedroom. It would now be considered a closet! We had bunk beds. I was on the top bunk, my brothers Henry and Michael were on the bottom. And the dog was under the bed. I'm the oldest, then Henry and Michael, and about twelve years later, came my sister Jennifer and brother Joseph, who are almost like Irish twins only they're Polish.

I went to Our Lady of Czestochowa and then I went to Cardinal Cushing for high school. I went to Cardinal Cushing for a year and begged my mother to let me leave. I lied to the nuns and told them my mother didn't have the money, so I had to leave because I wanted to go Southie High with my cousins. I drove my mom so crazy she finally let me go to Southie High. She always said, "Worst decision I ever made." And she was right! I said, "Don't let your kids make the decision on their education until they're nineteen."

I became pregnant at sixteen. I was from a Catholic family, the oldest one and pregnant, and we're talking 1968. It was taboo back then, and I don't even think they let you stay in school if you had a baby. Of course I dropped out. I had a baby girl, Jodi, in July of 1968. Thank God for my mother and father because I was able to stay home with my child. My mother worked graveyard shifts at Boston City Hospital as a senior nursing assistant in the pediatrics ward, from 11 p.m. to 7 a.m. She would come in at 7:15 in the morning because it wasn't that far away again, you know? Jobs were close to home. I'd be sitting at the bottom of the stairs with this little baby in my hands not knowing what the hell I'm supposed to do because the baby wouldn't sleep. Oh, I had to prove everybody wrong and get married, and I did. And it was not good.

Once my daughter went to school, I went to get my GED. Then, when I applied for [the University of Massachusetts at Boston], I also tried to find out if there was anything that I could get and there was absolutely zero help there. Nothing. Returning Women's Studies at UMass was the only thing that helped me out.

UMass was very new then, yet it was leaking and it was sinking, and doing everything buildings aren't supposed to do. You walk through hallways, there were buckets all over the place. I can't believe that they build buildings like this, right on a beautiful bay with ocean breeze, but not one damn window opens. They used a ventilation system, but when it didn't work right everyone would get sick. Really—right on the bay and no natural airflow to any of the buildings!

I worked as a waitress from the age of sixteen. I worked many jobs in this profession, but I couldn't picture myself doing it the rest of my life. I wanted something better for myself and my daughter. So, I majored in accounting until I had a professor that absolutely turned me off. He was a graduate of West Point, and that's exactly how he directed his class and it was just awful, and that was the end of it for me. So, I just did business management.

Then, I went to work. I did an internship out of UMass Boston with the Boston Housing Authority. I was in Jamaica Plain in the Boston Housing Authority warehouse. While there, I revised the whole operations manual and eventually worked my way up within the housing authority and became a manager. They opened up positions called Rent Collectors and I did that. I worked at Franklin Field, Franklin Hill, Old Colony, McCormack, and Broadway. I had all five developments. Eventually I became a Manager II and then a Manager I at the McCormack development right across from Moakley Park. Ironic because I lived there, raising my daughter for a few years.

When my daughter went to high school, I moved out to Brighton and was living with my boyfriend at that time. We got married and eventually divorced. I stayed with my cousin for a while because I didn't have anywhere to stay and I didn't want to be back at my mother's. That's how I came back to Andrew Square. Andrew Square was always ... I don't know what words to use for it, but it was always like the poor child with the ripped clothes. We had a problem with Amtrak. We had a train crash into the overpass on Southampton Street. I don't know how many years that took to get it fixed. I mean, that almost took an act of Congress. Andrew Square never got its recognition as to what it is. I mean, Andrew Square is a gateway from Dorchester, the South End, all that. It is just like Broadway but it was never recognized as that. It was always ignored. I don't know if it was because the income in that area is a little lower than what it is up at City Point or whatever, but there certainly is a difference in the way that it was looked at and treated. Take my neighborhood more seriously, you know? It's a neighborhood. We have taxpayers. We have workers. We've been here for a long time and we'll continue to stay.

The quality of life has certainly gone down and it's going down because we have a great amount of addicts. I know it's a disease, but it spreads like a cancer and affects everyone's quality of life. They come right from over the bridge. I mean, there are times that I have seen women pushing baby carriages and are drooling more than the baby in the carriage. It's not good. It's very scary and I fear for the child. It's an epidemic that we need to look at differently because what we are doing is not working. We're hoping with the new developments that we have going into Andrew Square that things will change. We have two new buildings going in, both of them will have restaurants on the first floor right near the square. The more traffic, the more people, the more likely things will start to dissipate. Washington Village will be a huge magnet for betterment in this area.

I welcome new development, to an extent. Some of the old was crap, like the junkyard. Thank God it's gone. But some of the old is good. You always want the old because it's comfortable, you know? Chunky little stores but they were mom-and-pop stores. You know what I mean? They had character and camaraderie. We had Alex and Laura down on Woodward Street. I used to get down there and get half a pound of bologna. They sliced it by hand, you know, with a big knife. The pickles in the barrel. It was a tiny store, yet it had all good food and they knew everyone by first name. Try that at Stop & Shop!

We have a lot of new people moving in, and I just hope they get involved with their community groups for the good of the quality of life and their neighborhood. And there are developers who work well with the neighborhoods, and like I said we are not against these changes. We're mostly concerned with some of the size and density of the proposals. As H. G. Wells said, "Adapt or perish." The neighborhood is changing anyway, and we have to change with it!

Dave Nagle, Chairman
South Boston
Community Foundation

I worked for the phone company for thirty years. It was New England Telephone and Telegraph, then Nynex, then Verizon. I left just as they were going from Nynex to Verizon. I took an early buyout. When I left, I was the head of all data products for New England.

I graduated South Boston High School in May of 1969 and my mom said, "You need to get a job." I applied for a job, as everyone in South Boston, gas company, telephone company, Edison at the time. It was a steady job. They were never going out of business. Everybody needed utilities. And then if you were a little bit older, guys that I grew up with who were coming back from Vietnam were police and fire, but I was young for police and fire. The phone company called and said, "Yeah, come on in." They did a test and they said, "Yeah, we'll hire you."

I was seventeen years old. The funny part about it was when they went to place me, they said, "You can't drive a vehicle for us because you're too young. You have to be eighteen to be insured." So, they put me in the central office in downtown Boston. And I ended up getting my undergraduate degree and my graduate degree from them. They put me through school. I went to Northeastern for my undergraduate and I went to Cambridge College for a master's in education administration. Nights, weekends. And then I worked nights and then I'd go days. All different shifts. I worked five to twelve, I worked twelve to seven, I worked days, I worked them all.

I got my master's in '88, so I got my undergraduate, I probably got it around '80 because I went in the Air Force when I worked for them, too. I went into the Reserve because the only lottery I ever won in my life was the draft lottery. I was number four. This was 1970.

The lottery was in existence until, I think, '72. And a lot of my friends were going to Vietnam. I said, "I don't really want to do that." So, I joined the Reserves. But I ended up staying in for three years. I ended up becoming a regular. The phone company, they actually paid the difference in salary. My Air Force salary was, say, twenty-five bucks a month and I was making, say $400 with the phone company. They paid $375. I went away, but I stayed active in the phone company. When I came back, I had all that service counted. So, the three years I did counted. When I came back, there were new people working in the phone company. They said, "Who's this guy?" And they said not only who he is, but he's senior to you. They were like, "What?" Yeah. But that was a great program there. When I came back, they gave me a check. I got a check for $4,500 when I came back. Bought a new car.

It was a great company to work for. When I left, they didn't want me to leave. I was only forty-seven and they said we don't want you to leave. We want you. But they were buying Bell Atlantic which was in Philly and they could have said tomorrow go to Philly. My wife was a lifelong South Boston person. She wasn't going to uproot and move. Not like today where the millennials will move in a heartbeat. So, I took the out and I consulted around for a little bit. Then I was the head of voice and data communications for Boston public schools, which people don't understand was at the time the most wired public-school system in America.

[In the Air Force, I was stationed in] Lackland, San Antonio, and then up to tech school at Wichita Falls, which is on the Oklahoma border in Texas. And then I was in … I was everywhere, Wright Patterson. I was at Andrews in D.C. Wright Patterson is in Ohio. I was in Turkey for a little while. I was all over. I was a cryptographer.

[In the Air Force] I was promised tech school, which they gave me. I just thought it was better than toting a gun and being in a foxhole. So, it was a little of both. I got a taste of some tech in the phone company, so this was a little bit of maybe I can use my brain a little. I ended up with a top-secret clearance. To be in cryptography you had to have that. It was funny, they came and investigated me without my knowledge. So, they spend about fifty grand to investigate you. They come and knock on the neighbors' doors. "Does he ever beat his mother? Is he gay?" Which today you couldn't ask that question, but yeah because I guess they felt the enemy could … I'd reveal code to the enemy. I don't think I ever saw the enemy. Not one I knew anyway.

I was in what they call the Top Gun class, where they sent people on the cutting edge of data at the time in the '80s and '90s. So yeah, I was pretty fortunate. I know a little bit—enough to be dangerous.

I was born October 1951. The street I lived on burned down, which is Jay Street. The streets go I and K and there is no J, but there is a Jay, J-A-Y, in between. It was a little, little side street that had maybe six houses on it and a fire began. So, they were connected, these three were connected, those three were connected. The fire began on our side of the street, burned down our three and then those three. They ended up building a school on the property. Jay Street's still there, but it's dead-ended. So, we got emergency housing in what's now the West Broadway housing development and we stayed there until I was about twelve.

My dad was a Teamster, a truck driver. And my mom was a homemaker, but she worked. She always worked a job. She worked at a lot of bakeries and we had six kids, so she was always working on a different job. I was the oldest boy, third from the top, but the oldest boy. Two older sisters. That's what the housing projects back then were for. You were supposed to get on your feet, save some money, and move out. Nowadays, no one leaves, but back then, we did. My dad bought a house up on Second Street and then they ended up getting ... they never got divorced, but they ended up drifting apart and until the day he died, they never got divorced. They were separated for thirty-eight years, but never divorced. Catholic, I guess. And we ended up in here, in Old Colony [housing development]. I'm probably fourteen, fifteen. I was in the ninth grade.

When Bill Linehan got elected to city council in 2007, West Broadway was a ghost town. There was nothing on West Broadway. And during the day, it was all junkies walking around. And at five o'clock, it went just dead like a ghost town.

You go up there now, baby carriages, bicycles, people all hours of the day and night walking around, families. It's just been revitalized. And it started with getting one guy to put a little restaurant in and another guy to do this and then put some residences. People didn't realize, above all that retail, there were always residences. Always people lived upstairs. And people put money in there, now it's the most vibrant part of the town. That's what they need [in Washington Village]. They don't have any of that.

I owned a restaurant on Broadway. In 1986, I bought it. And in 1986 until 1996, Broadway was the same way. The methadone clinic was over at Frontage Road. In the morning, they'd get their methadone. They used to walk across the bridge and hang around in front of my little restaurant. And people would say, "Oh, those guys were in there drinking all day." No, they weren't. They were just the methadone people waiting for their ride home to wherever or do whatever. Now it's a hotel, ten restaurants. One or two guys take a chance and it's amazing what a little investment will do. And that's what [the Washington Village development] is really going to do.

When I was a kid, when I was hanging around there, there was a fruit stand that went right up the side of Old Colony Avenue. Those were three-deckers in that lot that are now the old Blockbuster. They burned down. But they called it "the Fruity." And that's where your mother would send you over to get tomatoes and potatoes and everything.

The Fruity was there. Going up Old Colony was Brother's gas station, then John's Sub Shop, and a Pizza-Pizza pizza place. And then after that, it's a liquor store now, but I don't think it was a liquor store when I was a kid. Then another sub shop. And then a Tom Thumb grocery store on the corner up there. And then up here was Billy Baker's. Billy Baker's was the most famous deli-convenience store in the neighborhood.

Everybody had an account. Your mother could send you up there, tell Mr. Baker "put it on my account" and then every Friday on payday, the mother would go down and pay. Baker's was milk and bread and small stuff, but it was a meeting place. Friends, all the people, everybody would be in there. Small place, but fresh deli, fresh meat. He would cut fresh meat.

[Dorchester Avenue and Old Colony Avenue] was all industrial. [Winthrop Printing] was here forever, the laundry [Crown Uniform and Linen] was here for a hundred years. Matter of fact, we all worked at the laundry. You could get a summer job at the laundry if you needed it. Not driving. We'd work inside. We had to pull the sheets off and fold them after they dried and that kind of stuff. It was all manual labor.

My mom worked at Joe's Sub Shop on Dorchester Avenue for twenty years. That's just on the same side as the station, down just before you get to the junkyard. Matter of fact, the guy that owned it, owned the junkyard.

When they put the convention center in South Boston, they passed legislation that said that for any gate show that's held there, South Boston would get fifty cents of the ticket. That's where the money comes from [for the South Boston Community Foundation]. So, every year, we open up to bid grants. You submit a grant. We go over the grant. We ask, "How does it benefit South Boston?" Over the years, we've had the veterans who wanted to go down to the World War II Memorial in D.C. one time. We funded the bus and that kind of stuff. And then the Vietnam Memorial up here wanted to put in Astroturf around the memorial so we did that.

I'm not a big fan of the housing in a lot of Old Colony. I think the area should have stayed industrial. This thing about putting housing and then having one commercial spot on the first floor, a thousand square feet. What are you going to put there? Insurance company? A lawyer? I'd like to see more mixed-use only because I don't think you can sustain all the housing.

**John Grygorcewicz
Holocaust Survivor and
Washington Village Resident**

I was born on April Fools' [Day]. Nobody wants to admit it, but I'll admit it because I fooled a lot of people with my life. 1943. I was born in Naliboki, Poland. It is now called Belarus.

In 1943, when I was four months old, the Germans invaded our area. We were put on trains as forced laborers for Germany. Both my mother and father. My mother made sure that they didn't separate us.

So, we were taken to Germany, my parents as forced laborers. We were in different towns. We ended up by the border close to Austria, a town called Rosenheim. We were in Westphalia. We were in Siegen. In Siegen we were bombed several times, all different camps. They were pushing us everywhere. We got moved so many times my mother once told me, she was hoping that the bombs would hit us, you know. But we stayed together. I think my grandmother was with us too. My father was put on a farm and my mother was put in an automotive factory. Someone was watching [the kids]. There was a Jewish kid that was with us. His name was Henryk. He was separated from his mother and his job was to take care of me. They were suspicious, the Gestapo, that he was not part of our family, but they were afraid of my grandmother because my grandmother wore all black and she wore a cross on her chest. They beat up my mother and father, but they would never touch my grandmother.

We were mostly in subcamps because I think the main camp, this was what my mother once said was that Dachau, you've heard of Dachau, which was close to the Austrian border, was overcrowded. So they had subcamps.

I could name all the diseases I had. I had no front teeth 'cause I didn't get vitamins A, B, C, or D, or whatever it was at the time. In England I went to all the doctors for treatment. Finally, in 1950, I got my front teeth.

[I got to England after] the troops came in, when the Allies came in, in 1945. When we saw that the Allies were coming, all the gates were left open. So, we were traveling through Austria, I think about two weeks, then we start heading toward Italy. We followed the people, we didn't know where we were going, we just followed the crowds. Mostly walking. Austria was still part of the German empire. So, we moved at night. I used to make a lot of noise, my mother used to tell me. My sister was born in February of 1945 so there were two kids now.

My father's father owned a lot of land and livestock and made a good living selling the lumber. My family was rich. My father was illiterate. He never went to school. He could do the numbers, but he couldn't read. I tried to teach him, my mother tried to teach him. He went as far as the fourth grade. I tried to teach them in class when I was six years old. He wasn't interested. But he spoke and understood seven different languages. Nowadays, they would call it "street smarts."

We stayed [in Austria] for two weeks, two or three weeks. Then we went to Italy. We were walking through the main square of Milan, guess who's hanging upside down with his girlfriend? Mussolini. I didn't see that. My mother and father saw that. And the Italians were very good to us. They were fighting the Fascists and all of that. The Italians were starving just like us. We were looking for food all the time. We were in Italy for about four months. Then we went to France and we were in France for about eight months.

While we're in France, my mother finds out my uncle is serving with the British Second Corps in England. So, the Red Cross comes to my parents in France and says, "I found a Peter Grygorcewicz, in the Polish Corps with the British Second Army." He says, "We have to move all you people. Do you want to go to England?" Why not? We're in France, let's go to where our relatives are.

So, we get to Dover, England. I think it's November 1946. As soon as we get off the ship, we're all quarantined. My mother is in bad shape. My father and me and my sister are in bad shape. So, the doctors get a hold of us. They put me and my sister in a hospital and first thing they give us is cod liver oil, because of all the vitamins. After a while they put us in a camp. This was Hiltingbury, Hampshire. So, in England, I'm six years old, I'm in a Polish school, they didn't want me to stay there because I'm not learning the English language. So next thing they do is they put me in an English school. It's 1950, there's a lot of resentment, the British wanted all the Polish out of England. So, I used to take a bus to school in Eastleigh. Who's waiting for us? British kids. Waiting to beat us up. As a group we could fight them. One day a big group awaits us; they start a fight; I get beat up. Blood is pouring out of my head. I rush home. My mother, she was studying to be a dietitian in Vilnius, it's Lithuania now. It used to be part of Poland. A nail sticking out of my head, blood is pouring out. Thank God my mother was studying to be a dietitian. She puts iodine, bandages all over me. The hospital was too far to travel. So, this was our welcome to England.

I was in England from '46 to '54. We had freedom; we had land. Trucks used to bring the fresh produce to the camp once a week, the milk, the heat, supplies. We had a small vegetable garden, we also raised rabbits and chickens. That was our main food supply. They took care of us, but they start jacking everything up. If you wanted electricity, they put in meters, you wanted heating you had to pay for this. So, for four to five years we're trying to emigrate to America, Australia, or Canada. We go to the American embassy in London in 1954 with the family to go over to America because my grandmother ... my grandmother didn't leave with us when we left, she was still in Germany. So, with her daughter, they migrate to America ahead of us, several years ahead of us. I don't know the exact date. So, we get a letter that we've been approved to leave for America. This is in April 1954.

So, we stopped at Ellis Island. We get off at Ellis Island, they were closing Ellis Island. I think we were the last ship that came in. I found out later, actually, Ellis Island would close permanently in November 1954. So, we get off, they check our records and they put us on a train from New York to South Station.

You couldn't come to America unless you had a sponsor. You couldn't go on welfare. You had to have a job waiting for you. You could not be a burden in America. You had to have a sponsor; you couldn't go on welfare. That was stressed to us at the American embassy. My aunt, my father's sister, was here. She was in South Boston. I still live in the same house. I was an eleven-year-old kid.

They got us an apartment on Woodward Place. I'm still at the same address. April 20, 1954. We come in, we turned on our lights. I look—what's that stuff crawling? Cockroaches all over the place. Cold water, flat black stove. The toilet was on the second floor. The third floor had no toilets. You had to use the toilet on the second floor with the other tenants. So, I said to my mother, "We left England for this dump?" I said, "I want to go back to England."

My mother started crying. She wanted to leave my father. But then my mother finds out she was pregnant with two kids, with twins, we couldn't go back. So, we were stuck here. Rent was $15 a month then. Everything was falling apart, so there was nobody that was going to rent an apartment to a family of six kids so we were stuck. We had to fix everything up. The windows were leaking. It was infested with mice. So, the first few weeks here we went and got a cat. I called her Fluffy. What a mouser. Once I caught her with a mouse in her mouth and one under her paw. You don't find cats like that.

So, the first church I saw, we were enrolled at the Polish church. But I said this one [Saint Monica's] is closer, I'll go there. So, I go to church and, after Mass, I wanted to see what South Boston looks like. I think it was my first or second week. So, I'm walking by on Old Colony Avenue. I had the short pants on walking by with a friend I just met, all of a sudden about twelve, thirteen kids with sticks come running out of the project hollering, "Get the British, get the British."

I had the shorts on, they pounced all over me. I had a black eye, scrapes all over me while I'm on the bottom. I started hollering, "I'm not British, I'm Polish!" Those kids didn't listen. Finally, a woman walking by broke up the flight. Welcome to America. I was eleven years old. I got the hell knocked out of me because I had short pants on.

So, the next day I go to St. Mary's School because I was enrolled in the fifth grade. The nuns asked me, "What happened?" I said I was marked by kids coming out of the project because I looked British and I had these short pants on. So, the sister says to me, "Well we can't let that happen again." So, she takes up a collection so I could get some long pants so I don't get beat up again going to school. The kids in the South Boston projects hated the British, remember. There was a lot of resentment. The Irish hated the British.

My father found work in the paper mills as a laborer. My father worked as a laborer for most of his life because he couldn't read. He was considered illiterate, so my father had a tough time. My mother had two jobs as a cleaning lady in town and as a cleaning lady for a judge in the South Boston court. So, we had low, menial jobs.

Andrew Square was completely Polish. The Irish help the Irish. The Italians help the Italians. The Polish won't help the Polish. They want to be better than you.

I went to English High School. My father, when he was working, he got a slipped disc. He broke his back and he couldn't make it. So, I used to help him when he used to pick up the wastepaper at John Hancock. I used to get up, at times, at three-thirty in the morning and go on a truck and help my father out. So, I used to be late all the time at English High School. I broke the tardiness record, the vice principal, Mr. Butters, told me. I said, "My first period is a study period, so why is that used against me?" Every time I was late, I had to stay after school. At that time, my family was more important to me than school.

Can I say something about Whitey Bulger? Whitey Bulger tried to rob me when I was at a gas station. I worked in 1984 pumping gas. He pulls into the station in a Cadillac with a .357 Magnum on the front seat. I didn't know it was Whitey at the time. He says, "Kid, give me $10," so I gave him $10 and he says, "Kid, have you ever been robbed?" I was forty years old at that time. I says, "Look, you idiot, I'm not no kid. I'm forty years old," so he smiled, gave me the $10 and drove away. So, I asked the lady in the other lane, I said, "Who was that nut?" She says, "Don't you know that was Whitey Bulger?"

I could tell you another short story on Whitey Bulger. My brother was a short order cook at Jackman's at Andrew Square. Police used to come in and order breakfast, it was $4 or $5 there, but there was this one policeman that didn't want to pay. So, my brother one day, my brother was over six feet, so he tells the policeman, you got to pay. So, the policeman grabs the ticket, he walks away. So, my brother grabs a hold of it, the policeman had no intention of paying, so he throws the eggs and the bacon right out. And who comes in the next day? Whitey Bulger. So, he says, "I heard you had a problem here?" He says, "Yeah, your cops don't want to pay." My brother was kind of daring. Whitey says to him, "How much does he owe?" My brother says [he owes] a lot of money for not paying. So, Whitey says, "You won't have any more problems 'cause my cops get enough money." So, you can put two and two together. What was going on then, and this was in Andrew Square, in the late '60s, '70s, and '80s.

Arthur Spilios, George Spilios, Plato Spilios, and Joe Mulvey
Crown Uniform and Linen Service

Arthur Spilios: My name is Arthur Spilios, and I'm the CEO of Crown Linen Service.

George Spilios: I'm George Spilios, co-president of Crown, as well as Arthur's nephew.

Plato Spilios: I'm Plato Spilios, also co-president, Arthur's son. George and I are fourth generation.

Joe Mulvey: Joe Mulvey, I'm director of operations at Crown. I've been there for thirty-six years. Not part of the family.

Arthur Spilios: You are part of the family.

Joe Mulvey: Indirectly.

Plato Spilios: Not by blood, but yes, you are, Joe.

Arthur Spilios: My father told me that the building was originally a factory that made shell casings for World War I. My grandfather founded the firm. Everybody that started in our industry never had a laundry. They either did things at home and eventually found a laundry to do the work for them, and as they grew, or they would put a laundry together to do their own work, to control the quality and the service. Buying this

building, I don't know who we bought it from, but it was purchased, I think, in the early 1930s or the late 1920s.

My father found the building, and the building was much larger than what we needed, because we were a very small company, and they assembled the laundry there. We did work for around fifteen or twenty other small linen suppliers. They all had stalls in the building, and we would process all the work and do the ironing. Just wheel their merchandise down to their cubbyholes or their stalls.

They had their own little family businesses. It was kind of like Quincy Market back in the old days, when you remember the old meat shops in there and everything. It was like that. As they grew, they left us, and as we grew, we needed the space for ourselves. So, this is where the foundation of the company started, where we had our first laundry.

Being born in 1939, going back right around when I was eleven or twelve years old, I would go with my father to work, sometimes on punishment duty by my mother, to get me out of the house, but I spent an awful lot of time with my dad. We were living in Belmont, Mass.

What I remember the most about it is the snowstorms. Because when we had a snowstorm, the most important thing was to get the trucks out, and I would go in with my father, because school was out during a blizzard or a severe snowstorm. I was eleven or twelve years old. He would station me up this end of the street, the corner of Damrell and Dorchester Avenue. Then he would be down at this end, at Old Colony and Damrell. Here's what we had to do. The minute a city snowplow came up the street, because Damrell would never get plowed, and probably intentionally, because my father, we had this system going on.

So, I would stand at one end of Damrell Street, Dad would stand on the other end, and the minute a city plow would come, my instructions, and I was twelve, thirteen years old, was to get out and wave. I'd say, "We'll give you $50 or $25," which was a lot of money, "if you could make one sweep down the street." Of course, as they were making the one sweep down the street, depending on which end they were coming from, my father would either wave to me or I'd wave to him, and we'd run down and open the gates. Then we would give him another twenty bucks to come in and, you know, move the snow bank out of the way to get the trucks out. I mean, those are my first real memories, I can still see those snowplows, and there were always two guys in the truck, and the little yellow light blinking.

That was always a challenge to get the trucks out in South Boston. Subsequent to that, we were using the building primarily for ourselves with the exception of a small stretch during World War II where we were making some field jackets upstairs for Uncle Sam. My father got to know the neighbors better than I did. I knew the neighbors by name, like Dan Marr. My father used to talk about Mr. Marr. He liked Mr. Marr a lot. Then you had M&O Waste next to us. Joe remembers some of the names better than I do, but I remember very clearly the diner up at the end of the street, at the triangle across from Dan Marr, and there was a place, a slaughterhouse for chickens, where they had processed chickens.

It was kind of a tight little neighborhood. I don't recall any neighborhood associations or anything, where we all got together. But my dad knew all the neighbors on a first-name basis.

We may have sold rags to M&O Waste, but it was kind of a ratty part of town. I mean, the buildings were lousy. We always kept the building nice and neat and clean and there was a constant battle of picking up trash.

The attraction of the location was the fact that we didn't have any money, and the building, my father bought the building for $30,000. All the windows were broken on the back. Dad put the chimney up. They tore that chimney down [in 2017]. He loved boiler rooms, and we generated our own power. It was more space than we needed, but everything that we have came from there. It's one of millions of stories about this country.

Once I became old enough to, I would say the age of fourteen or fifteen, summers I was out on the routes with the route men, and learning the business, and then in the plant. The type of customers that we had, I would say, 75 percent food and beverage restaurants, and some motels. We didn't do hospitals at all.

Plato Spilios: We do now.

Arthur Spilios: When everybody started in the industry, most of us, most of these people of my grandfather's generation were immigrants. For one reason or another, they got into the industry. Either they became route people for someone like us, and then left and started their own companies, that happened. But the industry was very ethnic, initially. The Greeks went, the few Greek companies all went after their friends that owned restaurants, through the church. The Italian Bonanno, he went after all the barbershops. The Jewish companies, and I remember the faces because we bought fifty or sixty of these companies over the years, they were delicatessens and meat houses, you know what I'm saying? The Irish guys were going after the pubs. It was very ethnic.

Then by the time the 1960s came, everybody was crossing in, when the next generation came in, everybody, the ethnicity was lost and everybody was going after everybody else's customers. That's how it worked.

And it was a small industry. When I say small, if you look in the Yellow Pages, when we had Yellow Pages, there were ten pages of beauty parlors, but linen service companies, there were maybe only eight companies. So, we all knew each other. We would break bread once a year at the New England Laundry Association, and then beat the hell out of each other the rest of the year. So, we were in a building where there were mostly family laundry services that were in business thirty or forty years before our industry started. The whole idea of rental service started around the early 1900s, but there were laundries before that.

To get started, you either put a couple of washers and dryers into your garage, or you found a laundry to do the work for you. Then when you got to a certain size, you looked for a building and you—there were no regulations on pollution. Everything went down the sewer.

I think when I started in the company, it was about, we had about six routes and we had maybe twenty-five people in the plant, two or three people in the office. We have a census now of around 225 people.

What happened with the expressway, we had lower-cost areas coming into the city. They infiltrated Boston, and we infiltrated their areas, because it was very much easier to ... I remember doing the route going down to Providence. We had customers. I used to have to go down Route 1 with twenty-five red lights. It was a long haul. The roadbuilding helped everybody, everybody. The whole interstate system had a huge impact on our industry because we run trucking companies. I mean, we're a multifaceted industry. We have, we're called a service company, but, basically, we run a factory.

We had two plants. We had a plant in Fall River that processed some of our work, and we had South Boston. The Fall River plant came from an acquisition. We did not own that building, it was an old mill building, dilapidated, and it became unsafe. Roof leaking. It was something that we had to address the situation. Then at that, simultaneously with that period of time, the developer came that made us an offer on our [South Boston] building. And along with the offer, he made it very convenient when my brother and I talked about it. It was a question of, how long would it take to find a piece of land and build a plant? The gentleman said, "Look, you can stay in the building and give us nominal rent," which was like very, very cheap rent. He gave us enough time to do what we needed to do.

Joe Mulvey: We were outgrowing that building in Boston.

Plato Spilios: We were bursting at the seams.

Joe Mulvey: South Boston, everything included, office, everything, was forty-two or forty-four thousand square feet. This building [in Brockton] is ninety-four thousand square feet, and it's thirty foot clear [in height]. So, you get to use the whole cube, where down [in South Boston], you had to duck under things, where you're walking around. We had garments over your head, but you just had to duck when you went under them.

Arthur Spilios: South Boston was a very efficient plant, when you took what we were putting through the plant. Joe did a super job of keeping it very orderly and neat and clean. We had a lot of customers toured the plant, and they used to say, "Geez, we'd go into new buildings that don't look as nice as this." But it had its limitations — trailers that we had parked on the side, storage trailers that were just like cheap additions.

My strongest memory of the neighborhood itself? If you went up the street, right where Dorchester Avenue meets Damrell, there's a side, at a forty-five-degree angle, there's another street. There used to be a diner there. There's a little building that's still there, and next to it was a chicken place where they used to slaughter chickens. It was a pretty clean place. The doors would be open on a hot summer day, and you'd see the chickens coming down the conveyor belt all squirming and a guy there slitting their throats. Then you'd go into the diner, and you'd go and have a little lunch. And these guys that would come in with all these bloody frocks. You remember those things when you're sixteen, seventeen years old.

Plato Spilios: There was Farnsworth Fiber across the street. They'd recycle batting and material from furniture. Every once in a while, you'd just see them come out, flying out of the building with a fork truck. They'd have a big bale on it that was just smoking. You know, they'd have fires all the time in that place. Marr and Company, the forklift folks with the aerial cranes, were down at the end of the street. Behind us to the right was Winthrop Printing.

When I got out of high school, I moved back here, to Middle Street. Got an apartment with a buddy of mine. I used to go under the fence to get to work. The one thing I noticed, was that it was very segregated back in the '80s. Things were starting to change, I guess, but even being a white kid. I remember talking to the neighbors, and they'd just treat me like I was an outsider. Because I hadn't grown up in South Boston. Any rocks you had sitting around on the street, you want to make sure everything was clean all the time, because the kids would break the windows with rocks.

Joe Mulvey: That was my job when I started. Early '80s, every Monday morning, I fixed broken windows. Then during the week, I had to walk up and down the street and pick up all the rocks, so they couldn't break too many windows. Every weekend. Every Monday morning, there'd be burned cars in the Winthrop [Printing lot], behind the Crown building. There was a little garage there with no door, and there'd be one car or two cars, burned out. It was an industrial area, nobody sees anything. You got, you know, some three-deckers there, but they weren't calling the cops. In the middle of the day, I'm walking down the sidewalk to go out to this building, for one reason or another. There's a car in there up on blocks with two guys working on it. Taking all the parts off the cars. At one o'clock in the afternoon.

Brian P. Wallace
Former State Representative
for South Boston

I was Ray Flynn's aide for twenty-three years, when he was [state representative], city councilor, and mayor. I didn't go to Rome with him [when he was named ambassador to the Vatican] because I had just recently gotten married. So, I stayed here and I ran for state rep and I got elected and served four terms. I ran for the open seat and won, and that was 2002. [I represented] all of South Boston and a small portion of Dorchester out by Saint Margaret's [parish]. I served from 2002 to 2010. I worked for Ray from the time I was in college, 1972, until he left for Rome, which was 1993.

I was born [in 1949] at F and Fifth, right near the Boys Club. I was a club kid, and that's basically where I grew up, in the club. My father was a custodian, and, back in those days, your mother was home and she did the home stuff. And your father worked, I mean, all my friends' fathers worked two or three jobs. My father was a custodian, he was a fish cutter, he worked at a package store. So, I saw him Friday night. We used to watch the Friday night fights together, and that was my time with him that I could guarantee. And then we'd see each other on the weekends.

My father's whole life, he wanted to be a fireman. That was his dream. He was a sergeant in the war and he got wounded in Germany. He was in the infantry, and he had a big hole in his leg and they wouldn't take him. And it really kind of crushed him, it really crushed him. So, he did all these other jobs just for us, to make even. He worked his ass off for us, just to make sure that we were okay. Send us to Catholic school and all that stuff. I went to Monsignor Patterson, [and then to] Southie High.

I've written five books, and one of the books I wrote was called *A Southie Memoir*. And I listed that there were more bars and churches per capita in South Boston than anywhere in the country. We had fifty-one bars at one time, in one year. And we had probably twelve churches. I mean, it was just amazing. Everyone would get drunk and then would confess their sins.

I have one brother, [Eddie]. He's a retired Boston police captain. [He's] five years older. Eddie went to Vietnam, came back and got on the water and sewer commission, and then we had some political connections, we got him on the cadets and he became a policeman.

The first campaign I worked was for Johnny Powers, for state senate. And I was young, I was six, seven, I don't know. I was like a mascot. I'd get coffee, stuff like that. But my father was close to [former US Representative Joseph J.] Moakley and Powers, and all those guys, he was friendly. In those days Southie was so politically powerful. It stemmed from [former US House Speaker John] McCormack. You had the speaker of the House. And then you had Moakley, and you had [former State Senate President William] Bulger, you had Flynn, it just kept going. You just kept going with power, and they all had some powerful positions. Southie was the epicenter of political activity at that time.

There was a picture on the front page of the New York Times. I was ten. And I said to my dad, "I'm going to help Ted Kennedy against Eddie McCormack" [in his first run for the US Senate, in 1962]. And my father almost went crazy. He said, "You're not helping Ted Kennedy." He said, "Eddie McCormack's from South Boston, you're helping Eddie McCormack. You don't ever go against your own."

And I said, "Dad, but his brother's the president." He said, "You know his brother?" I said, "No." He said, "Well, I know Eddie McCormack. So, you go up and you help Eddie McCormack." So, I went up to the huge debate at South Boston High, the famous debate where McCormack said, "If your name was simply Edward Moore, instead of Edward Moore Kennedy, your candidacy would be a joke." So, I'm standing there holding a sign that says, "We'll back Jack, but Teddy isn't ready." Eddie McCormack came out of the car and saw me and came running over and said, "That's a Southie kid."

I was [at the Boys Club] all the time. I mean, I lived right directly across the street. I would come home, throw my school bags in my hall, and go right to the club. I was a basketball player, so I would stay there and watch Ray Flynn play, and all these guys. Oh God, Ray was amazing. I rebounded; I was his rebounder. He hit 114 foul shots one day in a row. But I mean, I learned so much from watching all those guys. They were the best. I wrote a poem about South Boston's best, and I said, "They all came through the club." And they did. [After Flynn went to Providence College], my father used to drive me to the Greyhound bus station. I'd go once a year, and I take the bus to Providence and Ray would pick me up at the station and take me to the game, and I'd sit on the bench, which was huge. And then I'd sleep in his room on a cot, and then he'd take me to the bus station the next day and I'd go home. I was probably twelve, thirteen. [My life was] all basketball all the time.

I broke all of Ray's records. I got a full scholarship to Loyola in Montreal. I averaged twenty-three points a game my senior year in high school. I played all day, all day. The ball was like part of my hand. I could just do things with the ball that other kids couldn't do. And I knew that was the only way I was getting to college; we didn't have the money. And I come home one day and said to my dad, "I'm going to Loyola in Montreal." [In 1974, Loyola College merged with Sir George Williams University to become Concordia University.] And he almost started crying. He said, "Brian, we don't have the money." I said, "No, no, no, no they're paying."

I had about fourteen scholarships. But see, at that time the freshmen couldn't play varsity [at US colleges]. This coach came down to see me play, and I scored thirty-eight against Hyde Park, who was number one in the state. And, he came in the locker room, he offered me a scholarship right then. And he said, "You'll start as a freshman." And I said, "What? Where do I sign?" I went up there and had a pretty good career. Oh God, I loved [Montreal], I loved it. Saint Catherine Street, my God.

[As far as the Washington Village/Andrew Square area is concerned], my relatives lived down there, the Gearys. They lived on Columbia Road. I used to visit them all the time. Kids from all over South Boston went to the Boys Club. Mostly the lower end. City Point [kids] really didn't. It was Old Colony, it was Old Harbor, it was D Street, it was lower-end kids. I knew a lot of the kids from Old Colony from the club. When I went down there, I would stay there for the day. We'd play stick ball, whatever. I just hung around. But I mean, no one really hung on the other side of Dorchester Street, that was no man's land, basically. Where the printing press was. That was just all deserted, like a dump. There was nothing there for us. A couple of my friends broke into the printing press. But you deal with all kinds in Southie, you just do. There was some activity on Middle Street, it had a good crew of kids.

Mutt Kelly, [owner of Kelly's Cork 'N Bull Tavern on Old Colony Avenue], he was a story in himself. I could write a book about him. He had hands that if you shook his hand, you lost yours. He was just a tough son of a bitch. And I remember going in there one day and asking him, I said, "Mr. Kelly, would you make a donation for the Pop Warner?" And he says, "Your name's Wallace, right?" And I said, "Yeah." He said, "Let me ask you, how many times you've been in here and bought a drink?" I said, "Never." He said, "Well, get the [hell] out of here." I mean, that's how Mutt Kelly was. He was a guy that you just didn't screw with, you just didn't. [His tavern] was a bucket of blood. A couple of people got killed coming out of there. I know at least three kids that got killed. It was a bad place. It was a place that you just didn't go in unless you had to.

I got hurt in college, I broke my ankle. It was pretty bad. They told me I wouldn't play again, because the only thing I had going for me was speed. This was in '69. I was a sophomore. I was feeling sorry for myself. I stayed in the house for six months. I mean, when I left, they had this big party for me, I was the number one scorer in the city and all this. So, then I'm coming home on my shield and it just didn't sit well. So, I stayed in the house for six months. And then Ray Flynn called me and said, "What are you doing?" I said, "Nothing." And so Ray said, "Get out. I want to see you in the gym tomorrow." So, I went over to the gym and Ray said, "Now knock it off. Now start dribbling the ball." I said, "I can't do anything." He said "You can dribble." So, I would dribble maybe for hours, just dribble. And then, I started running a little bit, and then Ray said to me, "Listen, Tommy Heinsohn called me today, he wants to know if you can play for the summer team, the Celtics summer team." They had a pro-am league.

That was the first year they had it, and we had Dave Cowens and a few other Celtics on our team. And I said, "I don't know if I can play." He said, "Well, the only way is to try." So, I played that summer, and I did pretty well. Then I said to Ray, "I'm done." He said, "What do you mean?" I said, "I can't get any better than that. I can't get any higher than playing for the Celtics." And he decided to run for rep that same summer. So, my whole life went from basketball to politics almost overnight. And he won, and I went with him and I stayed with him for twenty-three years.

David Pogorelc
Founder
Core Investments, Inc.

I'm originally from Minnesota, living in Boston, and working in the area of South Boston, that at one time was named Washington Village. My company, Core Investments, does real estate development, investment and development, and speculation. We improve properties, bring about a renaissance to properties, and improve the quality of life for other people.

Both parents are from Minnesota. My mother grew up in Minneapolis—my grandfather was an iron ore miner on the Iron Range in Minnesota, and my mother's father was a construction worker in Minneapolis. My parents met in Minneapolis, and they got married there. I was born there.

I've always owned real estate. I've been in the real estate business for thirty-five years or so. I did some brokerage when I was an independent agent when I got out of Bryant [University] for a couple of years. But I was buying real estate at that time anyhow. I started a real estate internship at Bryant. I got my real estate license at Bryant. But how it all started was really my mother. When I was in high school, I owned a contracting company, and I also owned a business buying and selling cars out of my parents' driveway, in Needham. We moved from Minnesota to Needham when I was in ninth grade.

At that time, my father worked for a security company, and he was in charge of sales. The security company made access systems; it was called

Synergistics. When you go into a bank building, you slide your card in and it opens the door, they had the patent on that. You'll see Synergistics on the bottom of that. But also security systems like card access. It could be for the Army. Some people have clearance to get into this building, and you need a card, and you get certain access to different people, so security in that way.

My mother always had a dream to own multiple two-families. So, finally, my father said, "Okay. Go out and buy a two-family." We were living in Needham and they bought a two-family for a rental property in Wellesley. She always wanted to do one, and my father didn't want to have anything to do with it because he was a corporate guy, and my mother's an entrepreneur. And then finally my father gave in and said, "Okay. Go ahead and do it." So, she went out and found a two-family in Wellesley, Queen Anne style, like four bedrooms on each side with a garage, walking distance to the commuter rail train station of Boston. Of course, I'm seventeen years old and I have all the answers, and I go to my mother, "Mom, you paid $124,000 for this?" Of course, five years later or whatever it was, they redid the kitchens and it sold for like 260, 280 grand. My father always said we shouldn't have sold anything. He was right. But now that place has to be worth $1.5 million or something.

So then when I was in college, my mother and I ... back then at hotels, they would have real estate seminars. You buy these cassette programs. You go there, they sell you. So then on the weekends you spent, back then, $200, $300 to buy it. She and I would go to these seminars. And then mother, she bought a two-family in Natick and then a single-family rental property in Needham, and then they ended up buying a small hotel on the Cape and my brother, Dan, ran it. And so that's how it started. For the last twenty-five years, my mother has owned a couple of gift shops on the Cape, so she's always been an entrepreneur.

I was taking these seminars, so then I ended up taking a real estate finance class, I got my real estate license when I was in college, and I started a real estate internship in college. And then I bought a two-family lot in Providence, which was the first property that I bought. I paid $7,000 for the lot, I sold it for $10,000. That deal was no different from what we do today, but my mother hand wrote the contract. Actually, I had just graduated college. And it's hand-written, and that's all you need. My mother's one-page hand-written note is all you really need.

I created this internship in Providence, and the owners of the company, they were a joke. They didn't have integrity and this and that. I sat in the back room, and there was this old guy, and I didn't call him John. I always called him Mr. Merolla. He was probably like 5'1", 5'2". He was retired, and he had nothing to do so he'd come in this real estate office just to BS with people. And he would come in and he had, I'll never forget it, an orange polyester tie that only came down about half way, and he had a sport coat, probably from the '60s. But he put it on and he came in, and he took a liking to me. He said, "Look, I'm going to teach you some things." And he said, "We got to get out of here."

So, he'd take me into city hall to learn how to look up property records, and then we'd go and do a drive-by. Rhode Island has a lot of plastic injection-molding businesses, and he owned one. And it was closed. He still owned the building. He said, "I want you to start this up and I'll do it, I'll finance it." And I'm like, "I'll go check it out, sure, Mr. Merolla." And so, I checked it out.

He just took a liking to me and he saw something in me probably similar to him. And he was trying to teach me things. And then one day he goes to me, "Come on. I want you to meet the mayor." And here I am, twenty-one years old or whatever, and I don't know this guy that well. The guy with the tie is telling me stories about this and that. I didn't know. I just thought he might be lonely. So, I said sure. Sure enough, we go down to city hall, he walks right into the mayor's office with me, and I meet the mayor.

I couldn't believe it. And then he started telling me other stories, and I kind of believed him, and then he said, "Look, I've got this two-family lot. And I built this street." And I'm like, "Okay." And then he took me to the lot. So that's the lot I bought, and he financed it.

I put down $2,000 and he financed $5,000. So, he goes to me—and I'll never forget this—he says, "I want you to meet my son, the general. And my other son runs the education system for the state of Rhode Island." And I don't know whether to believe him or not.

He says, "I want my son, the general, to write up the agreement." So, I said, "Okay." Well sure enough, we go downtown to meet the general. The general's an attorney. His son's an attorney. So, we go into his office, and his son is a general. His son is the highest ranking general in the state of Rhode Island. And I'm like, "Whoa."

So, we go into his office. And his son, who's this big burly military guy, was sitting in his office, big office. Mr. Merolla says to his son, "This is Dave. I want you to write up an agreement that he's going to buy the lot and I'm going to finance him; we're going to build a house together." And his son just lays into his father. "Dad, I don't want you working. What are you doing? Dad, you're not going to do this." And Mr. Merolla, like 5'1" with his little orange tie, says, "Look. I'm your father. You don't talk to me that way." And the general, the military bulldog, becomes like this little child out of respect for his father. He almost slouches in his chair, and he says, "Yes, Dad. I'm sorry, Dad." It was a beautiful story of respect the general had for his dad.

And then, of course, the general did write up the contract. We did do the deal, and it's also hanging on my wall.

And the general. You know what happened to him next? He was appointed Supreme Court justice for the state of Rhode Island. So that's my first deal. And it was a beautiful experience. That's why I have it hanging up on the wall. And here's an older guy that just took a liking to me and helped me out. And in that deal, like I said, now in today's deals you just add multiple zeroes, it's the same deal. The margins are the same. It's the same deal.

I ended up selling the lot. I didn't build on it. I sold it to a husband and wife. He was from Italy and he didn't speak English, and she was American, but she spoke Italian. And I sold it to them, and Mr. Merolla and I both went to the closing together, and we sold it to them.

I get the biggest kick out of building homes for first-time home buyers. It's not sexy, but it's extremely rewarding. Simple stuff, but everybody remembers their first home. At 1914 Washington Street in Boston, we condo-ed a building, and we were only selling to first-time home buyers for probably six to ten years. So, I went to the closing on this one buyer. They were from Romania. I honestly believe you can't get ahead in this country unless you own your own home. So here they are. I think she was a dentist. I don't think he was the dentist. Young married couple, and they said, "This is a really big day for us." And I'm like, "Yes, it is. You're buying your first home. Young married couple. Congratulations, it's the American Dream. Congratulations." And they said, "Yes, and this morning, we just got sworn in as American citizens."

I almost literally fell out of my chair. The American Dream. They were sworn in as American citizens and they're buying their first home on the same day.

In the beginning I'd paint the apartments, I'd do the landscaping. I would even, to save what at that time was $75, when I would sell one of these condos or sell a property, the attorneys wanted $75 to write up the deed. And I'm like, "It's too much money. I can't afford that. We're dealing in small dollar amounts." It meant something to me. So, I would go down, and again, learning from Mr. Merolla, I would go down to Registry of Deeds, I'd look up the former deed, I'd copy the former deed, I'd take out the names and I'd replace the names myself and type it up, save seventy-five bucks.

I had a private lender who we still work with. His name is Henry. I've done probably a hundred and some odd deals with him. And I met him when the market in the early '90s crashed, my credit was gone. I couldn't borrow from banks, plus banks weren't lending. So, I met this guy through an attorney, and this guy makes mortgages. He's a plasterer who made a few dollars and he now loans his money. He would finance me, not as a partner, but strictly as a bank. I pay probably double the bank's interest rate, but I was fine. I'm still fine with it even today to pay double. But there's no BS. It's just like, "Hi, I need X dollars, Henry. Thank you." One week later I have the money.

We still do residential. We've owned all different types of properties. Apartments, condos, homes, we've built subdivisions, owned a couple of marinas, industrial buildings. We own a sand and gravel operation. Industrial land, industrial property, land development, new home construction, that's probably it. Right now we have sixteen people, and we're hiring some more people. This year we'll probably have another four or five people. We own quite a bit of land in South Boston. We're the largest private landowner in South Boston. We have about twenty-seven acres in total. In Westminster we own land, which is a sand and gravel operation, but it's permitted for a million and a half square feet of commercial space. And, actually, we're working on a deal to sell some of the land right now. But other than that, everything's in Boston. Boston is the best city.

The first deal I did in South Boston was in the mid-'90s. And I didn't go back to South Boston until 2010 probably. Fifteen years. I bought a mortgage, and that's another thing we do. We're buying mortgages. And we bought a mortgage on a bankrupt company. That was Winthrop Printing. We bought the mortgage and we foreclosed. The property's vacant, the company's gone, and we foreclosed. And that was the first property in Washington Village. So, we bought that property.

I went to introduce myself to the neighborhood association saying, "We just bought this property. I just want to introduce myself." I said, "Hey, my name's Dave. We haven't figured out what we want to do with the property, but if you have any ideas, I'd love to hear them."

And that shocked the neighbors, because no developers do this. They just tell people what they're going to build here. They say, "Well we're allowed to do this, this, and that." I went to them and said, "What would you like to see here?"

And they told me, and I'll never forget it, they said, "We used to have four grocery stores in South Boston. Now there's only one. We are underserved with grocery stores. And, also, there's no place for the community to meet." And I said, "Okay." So, I went back and I started doing some drawings. And I showed them, I said, "Look, to do it right, I'm going to need more land to accomplish this." Because for a grocery store and a park, I realized two and a half acres wasn't enough. So, then I started buying up the other pieces, and the neighborhood became partners in this because we're helping them with their goals. They became very supportive of us as opposed to the big bad developer.

I started to deliver them what they wanted. I didn't have a plan of what I wanted yet. But I thought, "Okay. I'll come back to them, I'll show them the grocery store that they wanted, and I'll show a park that would be the community meeting space in my mind." And then to fill in how are we going to pay for all this, I would have to figure out, "Okay, it'd be apartments and condos. I'll figure that out later." You put your best foot forward.

I got my permits in '16 [for Washington Village]. We're going to come out of the ground this summer, 2020. And we took [Samuels & Associates] on as our partner.

And then we started buying up everything on the other side of the street. I always knew there was even more opportunity on the other side of the street, but I owned one property with a partner, 501 Dot Ave., but I didn't own anything else. And then in '16 I think I bought 371 Dot Ave. And then since then I've bought multiple pieces since to fill it all in. It will probably take us a year to two years to get all our permits.

That project, On the Dot, will be about 30 percent residential. Residential meaning apartments, condos, maybe fifty-five and older, maybe assisted living, and maybe hotel.

The image that comes to my mind when I think of Washington Village is a little kid flying a kite. We're creating a community where life is going to happen. To me, it's not about the buildings. The buildings are irrelevant. It's all about what's happening around those buildings. It's creating memories, it's creating experiences, human interaction. That's what we're doing.

If this works, we can do this all over the world. This isn't ego talking. It's not. What we're doing, and we're always ahead of the curve in everything we do, this is going to be replicated in many different places. It will. I just know it will, and it's tough to explain why.

We're creating a neighborhood within a neighborhood. I want to have a school, we're going to have a day care center, we're going to have all these things. We're building a community within a community. Our objectives are to improve the quality of life for others. God's peace.

Bibliography and Interviews

Alger, Arthur Martineau. *A Genealogical History of That Branch of the Alger Family Which Springs from Thomas Alger of Taunton and Bridgewater, in Massachusetts, 1665–1875.* Boston: Press of David Clapp & Son, 1876.

Cheney, Frank. *Boston's Red Line: Bridging the Charles from Alewife to Braintree.* Charleston, SC: Arcadia Publishing, 2002.

Cheney, Frank, and Anthony M. Sammarco. *Boston in Motion.* Charleston, SC: Arcadia Publishing, 1999.

Christian, Paul A. *South Boston On Parade: A History of South Boston's Evacuation Day and Saint Patrick's Day Parade. Boston*: Loving Boston Press, 2016.

Clarke, Ted. *South of Boston: Tales from the Coastal Communities of Massachusetts Bay.* Charleston, SC: History Press, 2010.

Conway, Lorie. *Boston The Way It Was: Pictures and Memories from the '30s and '40s.* Boston: WGBH Educational Foundation, 1996.

Gillespie, Charles Bancroft. *Illustrated History of South Boston. London*: Forgotten Books, FB&c, Ltd., 2017. First published 1900 by Inquirer Publishing Company (South Boston).

Heald, Bruce D. *Boston & Maine Trains and Services.* Charleston, SC: Arcadia Publishing, 2005.

Karr, Ronald Dale. *The Rail Lines of Southern New England: A Handbook of Railroad History.* Pepperell, MA: Branch Line Press, 1995.

Krieger, Alex, and David Cobb, eds. *Mapping Boston.* A Norman B. Leventhal Book. With Amy Turner. Cambridge, MA: MIT Press, 1999.

Liljestrand, Robert A. *The New Haven Railroad's Old Colony Division.* Ansonia, CT: Bob's Photo, 2000.

Loftus Jr., Patrick J. *That Old Gang of Mine: A History of South Boston.* South Boston: TOGM-P.J.L. Jr., 1991.

McCullough, David. *1776.* New York: Simon & Schuster, 2005.

Moore, Barbara W., and Gail Weesner. Back Bay: A Living Portrait. Boston: Century Hill Press, 1995.

Most, Doug. *The Race Underground: Boston, New York, and the Incredible Rivalry that Built America's First Subway.* New York: St. Martin's Press, 2014.

O'Connor, Thomas H. *South Boston My Hometown: The History of an Ethnic Neighborhood.* Boston: Northeastern University Press, 1994. First published 1988.

Pearson, Henry Greenleaf. *The Life of John A. Andrew, Governor of Massachusetts 1861–1865.* Boston: Houghton, Mifflin and Company, 1904.

Powers, John. *The Boston Handbook.* Illustrated by Peter Wallace. North Attleborough, MA: Covered Bridge Press, 1999.

Puleo, Stephen. *A City So Grand: The Rise of an American Metropolis, Boston 1850–1900.* Boston: Beacon Press, 2011.

Report of Study for a Section of the John F. Fitzgerald Expressway, Boston, Massachusetts. Boston: Clarkeson Engineering Company, Inc., 1954.

Sammarco, Anthony Mitchell. *Dorchester.* Charleston, SC: Arcadia Publishing, 2005.

Sammarco, Anthony Mitchell. *South Boston.* 2 vols. Charleston, SC: Arcadia Publishing, 1996–2000.

Sammarco, Anthony Mitchell. *Then & Now: South Boston.* With contemporary photographs by Charlie Rosenberg. Charleston, SC: Arcadia Publishing, 2006.

Seasholes, Nancy S. *Gaining Ground: A History of Landmaking in Boston.* Cambridge, MA: MIT Press, 2003.

Seasholes, Nancy S., ed. *The Atlas of Boston History.* Chicago: University of Chicago Press, 2019.

Simonds, Thomas C. *History of South Boston, formerly Dorchester Neck, now Ward XII. of the City of Boston.* Boston: David Clapp, 1857.

Toomey, John J., and Edward P.B. Rankin. *History of South Boston, (its past and present) and Prospects for the Future, with Sketches of Prominent Men.* Boston: printed by the authors, 1901.

Tsipis, Yanni. *Boston's Central Artery.* Charleston, SC: Arcadia Publishing, 2000.

Vrabel, Jim. *When In Boston: A Time Line and Almanac.* Boston: Northeastern University Press, 2004.

Warner Jr., Sam Bass. *Streetcar Suburbs: The Process of Growth in Boston (1870–1900).* 2nd ed. Cambridge, MA: Harvard University Press, 1978.

Interviews Conducted

Joey Karas, Karas & Karas Glass Co., May 8, 2019

Robert Allison, Suffolk University history professor, May 15, 2019

Linda Zablocki, Andrew Square Civic Association and neighborhood resident, July 10, 2019

Dave Nagle, South Boston Community Development Foundation, July 17, 2019

Arthur Spilios and others, Crown Uniform and Linen Service, Sept. 11, 2019

John Grygorcewicz, Holocaust survivor and neighborhood resident, Dec. 18, 2019

Brian P. Wallace, former state representative from South Boston, February 28, 2020

Dave Pogorelc, Core Investments, February 28, 2020

Acknowledgements

Though writing is a solitary enterprise, no book is ever the product of just one (or in this case, two) authors. All authors need help in creating and shaping a project, researching it, and turning it from idea into reality.

This book would not have come about without the help of many hands. First and foremost is the founder of Core Investments, Dave Pogorelc, who commissioned the book and championed it throughout the process. This book would not have happened without the support of Dave's entire team at Core, including Tom Palmer, who patiently supervised its making from the outset.

Suffolk University historian Robert Allison, who also serves as president of the South Boston Historical Society, sat patiently through interviews and shared his insights on the South Boston neighborhood with us.

We had research assistance from many dedicated professionals in Boston, who helped us locate and identify relevant maps, photographs, and news items. The librarians and archivists at the Boston City Archives, the Boston Museum of Science, Northeastern University's Archives and Special Collections Center, Digital Commonwealth, and the Norman B. Leventhal Map & Education Center of the Boston Public Library all made valuable contributions to this project, and researcher Carol Beggy turned up many valuable stories about Washington Village in contemporary newspapers. Author Tina Cassidy and her former colleagues at InkHouse graciously shared the information they compiled on Washington Village.

Laura DiNardo, a graduate student at Columbia University and daughter of one of the authors, copy edited the manuscript with style and grace. Any errors are, of course, the responsibilities of the authors alone.

Book designed by Perugi Design, Boston

Cover designed by Greenspace, London

Original photos by Shun Liang Photography, Boston

Original maps by David Butler

Printed by HFGROUP AcmeBinding, Charlestown

Supervising Editor Tom Palmer, Tom Palmer Communication

Richard Kennedy

Born and raised in Brighton, Massachusetts, Richard Kennedy graduated from Bentley College (now Bentley University), majoring in accounting and minoring in commercial law. He worked for most of four decades in the commercial banking industry in the City of Boston, prior to joining Core Investments as a financial consultant, specializing in the acquisition of defaulted commercial mortgage loans. He has two daughters and three grand-daughters and lives in downtown Boston. (Mr. Kennedy passed away in May 2021.)

Bennie DiNardo

Bennie DiNardo was an editor at The Boston Globe for more than 20 years. As deputy managing editor for digital, he launched BostonGlobe.com and oversaw the editorial operations of the Globe's website and that of its sister website, Boston.com. He also served as a night copy editor, an assistant editor at the Globe magazine, and as deputy business editor. Prior to joining the Globe, he served as State House reporter and then as editor of the Boston Business Journal and was a staff writer at Worcester Magazine. A 1979 graduate of Cornell University, he also earned a master's degree from Yale Law School in 1986 after participating in the school's Fellowship in Law for Journalists.